CAREER CRIMINALS

Volume 30
SAGE RESEARCH PROGRESS SERIES IN CRIMINOLOGY

SAGE RESEARCH PROGRESS SERIES IN CRIMINOLOGY

Published in Cooperation with the American Society of Criminology
Series Editor: **MICHAEL R. GOTTFREDSON,** *State University of New York at Albany*
Founding Series Editor: **JAMES A. INCIARDI,** *University of Delaware*

VOLUMES IN THIS SERIES (editor / title)

SAGE RESEARCH PROGRESS SERIES IN CRIMINOLOGY
VOLUME 30

CAREER CRIMINALS

EDITED BY
Gordon P. Waldo

WITHDRAWN

Published in cooperation with the
AMERICAN SOCIETY OF CRIMINOLOGY

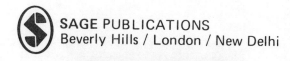 **SAGE** PUBLICATIONS
Beverly Hills / London / New Delhi

For information address:

SAGE Publications, Inc.
275 South Beverly Drive
Beverly Hills, California 90212

SAGE Publications India Pvt. Ltd.
C-236 Defence Colony
New Delhi 110 024, India

SAGE Publications Ltd
28 Banner Street
London EC1Y 8QE, England

Printed in the United States of America

Library of Congress Cataloging in Publication Data

Main entry under title:

Career criminals.

   (Sage research progress series in criminology ; v. 30)
   "Published in cooperation with the American Society of Criminology."
   Papers presented at the 1982 meetings of the American Society of Criminology.
   Contents: Professional theft / Julian B. Roebuck and Gerald O. Windham—On the grift at the Superbowl / James Inciardi—God and the Mafia revisited / Jay S. Albanese—[etc.]
   1. Crime and criminals—United States—Congresses. 2. Organized crime—United States—Congresses. I. Waldo, Gordon P. II. American Society of Criminology. III. Series.
HV6789.C37 1983   364'.973   83-17855
ISBN 0-8039-2168-3

FIRST PRINTING

CONTENTS

Gordon P. Waldo

Florida State University

INTRODUCTION

The papers for this volume were all presented at the 1982 Meetings of the American Society of Criminology and their quality attests to the continuing improvement in the research being presented at the national meetings. This volume was prepared because a large number of the papers presented dealt with specific types of criminal behavior, many of which appeared to develop out of a typological approach to crime. Unfortunately (or fortunately), there were many more good papers than could be incorporated into this book of readings, and a number of excellent papers had to be eliminated either due to length or subject matter as the scope of the volume was narrowed from typological studies in general to a more specific subset of papers.

The typological approach has met with mixed reactions in terms of its impact on the field of criminology. Several excellent books have been written utilizing a typological approach, with three of the better-known works being Gibbons, *Society, Crime, and Criminal Careers;* Clinard and Quinney, *Criminal Behavior Systems: A Typology;* and Inciardi, *Careers in Crime.* Typologies have an inherent appeal, in that they permit us to order and classify different types of crime and criminals into coherent categories, which in turn forces us to recognize the similarities and differences among various types of crime and criminals. This is advantageous, in that it logically leads to explanatory models and theoretical explanations that are consistent with the empirical regularities observed in the typological categories. Microtheories of different types of crime, combined with midrange theories that attempt to integrate diverse microtheories, could greatly expand the theoretical base in criminology.

7

However, the major thrust in criminological theory in recent years has been at the macro or grand theory level with little concern for the micro level. Critical criminology, while providing important insights into many questions dealing with the study of crime (some of which are addressed in the chapters in this volume), has diverted attention from attempts to develop theories dealing with specific types of crime. This has occurred despite the fact that Quinney has been a major contributor to the study of typologies as well as the development of critical criminology. It would appear that critical criminology had more impact on his study of typologies than the typological approach had on critical theory.

The present book of readings does not attempt to develop a typology per se, and none of the readings is specifically concerned with an overall typology of crime. What these readings do is to add specific details to our knowledge about three categories of crime that have been included in most of the typologies that have been previously developed—namely, professional, organized, and corporate crime. These three areas have been frequently incorporated into the general category of "career crimnals." Some typologies would also include other types of career criminals—such as, "occupational crime" (white-collar crime), "political crime," and "ordinary career crime"—within the general category; but most criminologists would probably agree that the three types of crime included in this set of readings clearly represent a major portion of the problem of crime as it exists today.

While each of these types of crime can be thought of as a distinct entity, they are not completely independent of each other. Professional crime and organized crime might interrelate in several ways. For example, the money for planning and pulling off a big job by the professional criminal may come from a loan shark affiliated with organized crime, or the fence used by "heavy professionals" in disposing of the proceeds from a big hijacking may be a part of organized crime. To the extent that organized crime takes over legitimate business, the link between organized crime and corporate crime becomes obvious. In addition, if a politician is receiving graft from someone in organized crime or a corporate official, then political crime, corporate crime, and organized crime can become intertwined. Indeed, as the chapter by Block and Scarpitti suggests, for some types of crime, it may not always be clear whether it should be categorized as corporate crime or organized crime, but the political implications of how it is perceived and labeled may be of considerable consequence.

The first two chapters in the volume deal with professional crime and are written by two of the foremost scholars in this area. The article by Roebuck and Windham builds on the earlier work of Roebuck and discusses the changing nature of professional crime and the fact that some criminologists are prepared to abandon the concept altogether. They reject this position, although noting that there is little agreement among criminologists concerning the definition and scope of professional crime. Their chapter provides a detailed review of the theoretical and empirical literature on professional crime, indicating that part of the difficulty involved in resolving some of the issues lies in the fact that different approaches, semantics, conceptualizations, and methodologies have been used in various studies, which has in turn resulted in different findings and conclusions. The authors suggest that the best way to proceed in future research would be to "return to a more elastic and extended version of Sutherland's behavior system approach" and for researchers to make "phenomenological studies of successful professional criminals in the open."

The second chapter, by Inciardi, focuses on a specific form of professional crime: the pickpocket. It represents a continuation in a series of studies conducted by Inciardi and perhaps epitomizes the type of research called for by Roebuck and Windham. Over a period of years Inciardi has interviewed a number of professional pickpockets or "class cannons," and the study presented here is concerned specifically with grift at the Super Bowl. He gives a brief description of several of his "cannons" and then discusses why the Super Bowl represents a prime occasion for the pickpocket. Inciardi concludes that the class cannon is slowly disappearing and discusses the rationale underlying this observation.

The next set of articles is concerned with organized crime, but their approaches and subject matters differ considerably. Albanese addresses the question that was examined earlier by Daniel Bell, Gordon Hawkins, Joseph Albani, and others which might be cryptically phrased the "myth of the Mafia." The basic question concerns whether or not there is a nationwide criminal conspiracy (Mafia, La Cosa Nostra, Syndicate, Black Hand, etc.) that controls organized crime in the United States. Following the lead of Hawkins, who analyzed the testimony of Valachi several years earlier in addressing this question, Albanese examines the testimony of Jimmy Fratianno in a similar manner. Fratianno's testimony was seen by some as more important than Valachi's because he was supposedly a high-ranking member of an organized criminal group and his testimony resulted in the conviction of several members of organized crime. Albanese concludes that Fratianno's "testimony sheds little light on an accurate understanding of organized crime" and discusses the "power of ideological beliefs in preventing the reception of new evidence inconsistent with prevailing views."

The fourth chapter by Lupsha is an attempt to use "social network analysis" in the study of a specific group of organized criminals, the "New Purple Gang," who are involved in narcotics distribution. This gang operated in a section of New York associated with organized crime and had blood ties to earlier generations of organized criminals, which permitted an examination of the "ethnic succession" hypothesis. Lupsha uses demographic and other data obtained from rap sheets and a form of sociometric and age cohort analysis in developing networks among the gang members. He is concerned with testing the accuracy of law enforcement intelligence information and also with examining the structure of this particular group.

Mieczkowski contributes the fifth chapter, which is also concerned with organized crime, but the methodology is quite different from each of the preceding articles. Each of the articles on organized crime might be called a case study, but they have used totally different kinds of data. Whereas Albanese used transcripts from court hearings and Lupsha used police rap sheets for his data, Mieczkowski used serendipitous participant observation and field methods for his data. He is concerned with testing the structural versus the process approach to organized crime and did a cross-cultural study by examining an organized criminal syndicate on one of the Caribbean islands. The "Raz boys," as the group is called, play both a legitimate and illegitimate role in the community, and the organization is described in nonbureaucratic, nonethnic terms and is said to have an informal leadership structure. Mieczkowski concludes that the process model is more appropriate than a structural model in understanding the Raz boys.

The subject of Block and Scarpitti's chapter is on the border between organized and corporate crime. Their study concerns the illegal disposal of hazardous waste, an area of study that would not have existed a few years ago. The authors note that this topic has been treated as a form of white-collar (corporate) crime in the literature and by enforcement agencies; however, they challenge this classification and suggest that it might be more appropriately considered a form of organized crime. Using secondary data from published reports prepared by government officials, they show that the hazardous waste industry in New

Jersey has been under the control of organized crime rather than legitimate business entrepreneurs and that efforts have been made, for political reasons, to divert attention from the role organized crime has played. The insidious nature of this labeling effort and the impact it has on enforcement practices, public perceptions, and criminological research is explored by the authors.

The final chapter clearly falls into the category of corporate crime as Cubbernuss and Thompson examine the implications of the Ford Pinto case. They use secondary data to argue that the criminal justice system is inadequate in the control of corporate crime. They report on the internal memorandum from Ford that indicates a rational decision-making process which led to the decision to pay the families of anticipated victims of the Pinto rather than cure the defect in the car because it would be more cost-effective. The authors proceed to examine the criminal court case of Indiana v. Ford Motor Company to illustrate the failure of the criminal justice system in controlling corporate behavior. The implications for overlap between political crime and corporate crime are also implicit in this article.

Although the chapters in this volume are quite diverse in method and approach, clearly a number of common themes bind them together. The most important is that each makes a contribution to some aspect of our understanding in the area of career crime and criminals.

Julian B. Roebuck
Gerald O. Windham

Mississippi State University

1

PROFESSIONAL THEFT

Professional theft as discussed in this chapter is synonymous with the more generic construct professional crime, and designates the illegal taking by a professional criminal of another's property without said victim's knowledge and/or informed cooperation. A wide range of ever-changing criminal pursuits are included—for example, professional "heavy crime" (burglary, robbery) as well as professional sneak theft, shoplifting, pickpocketing, confidence games, forgery, and other false pretense crimes such as illegal medical quackery and credit card theft. No longer is it feasible to separate for analysis traditional theft (e.g., confidence operations) from "heavy" crime because research over the past 40 years indicates the versatility of criminal careers that is personified in the life of the career hustler (Walker, 1981).

Professional crime is career crime committed by professional criminals. Many criminals have criminal careers of sorts in terms of receiving money from criminal pursuits and demonstrating some kind of patterned criminal behavior within a particular time frame, but such minimum criteria do not specify professional criminals. Many criminologists substitute the terms "career criminal" and "career crime" in lieu of "professional criminal" and "professional crime." Some of these, among others, claim that very few professional criminals remain on the scene because of changed social conditions—for example, the improvement in police methods, changes in the economic system, and the elimination of the fix (bribing some official) that ensures the thief's freedom from the court system (Jackson, 1972; Inciardi, 1975). Some of these criminologists would even remove the term "professional criminal" from further discussion.

The position herein opposes such views. Professional crime is career crime, but not all career crime is professional; professional criminals are career criminals, but not all career criminals are professional criminals. Professional criminals and professional crime endure; and though the content of crime is ever changing, the form of professional crime persists. Many criminologists of another persuasion, however, have made formidable contributions to the field of criminology.

Inciardi (1975: 5-75) documents the conditions necessary for the practice of professional crime that have existed since the beginning of the industrial order. Crimes pursued as occupations in the West began in England with the decline of the feudal system (1350-1550) and the development of capitalism. In order to survive, those displaced from the occupational structure invented alternative forms of economic subsistence (including criminal enterprises) within the new urban centers created by industry and commerce. Some of those uprooted joined jugglers, minstrels, gypsies, robbers, poachers, and bandits to form an urban criminal subculture. Accounts of professional crimes in England date from the fifteenth and sixteenth centuries when war and economic change forced many peasants off the land. A variety of tracts, pamphlets, and ballads depicted the lives of rogues, vagabonds, and thieves in the Elizabethan period.

Henry Mayhew (1862) explored and wrote about the criminal class in London's slums in the middle of the nineteenth century, describing numerous types of criminal and deviant lifestyles, including prostitution, theft, swindling, conning, fencing, burglary, robbery, begging, pickpocketing, shoplifting, forgery, embezzling, and gambling. He derived a rough classification of thieves ranging from the very proficient and successful to the habitual unskilled type.

Professional crime was firmly established in England during the eighteenth and nineteenth centuries and subsequently exported to the United States, where it emerged as a subculture (or contraculture) in the larger urban areas during the nineteenth century (Inciardi, 1975: 46-70). Heavy career crime spread rapidly throughout the United States with the westward movement and the economic development of the frontier (Barlow, 1981: 138-199). In England, the United States, and elsewhere, crime as an economic way of life has prospered in a supportive environment and has followed legitimate business, "often filling in the gaps left by other forms of commerce" (Quinney, 1975: 244-248).

There is no full agreement among criminologists or the police about the definition of professional crime or professional criminals (Walker,

1981). A plethora of definitions and secondary analyses is extant in criminology textbooks (Sykes, 1956: 108-119; Vetter and Silverman, 1978: 129-163; Conklin, 1981: 337-361), the criminal's own account (Martin, 1952: Rettig et al., 1977), and researchers' field notes and observations (e.g., see Lemert, 1958; Cameron, 1964; Roebuck, 1967; Roebuck and Frese, 1976; Gould, 1966; Irwin, 1970; Letkemann, 1973; Klockars, 1974; Pruis and Irini, 1980). However, as Walker (1981) demonstrates, only a few empirical studies comprise the data base for theories about professional crime.

Before examining the literature, we submit the following definitions of the professional criminal and professional crime based primarily on Roebuck's studies of prison inmates and criminals in the open (Roebuck, 1967; Roebuck and Frese, 1978). By way of delimitation, the following types of crime and criminals are excluded: organized criminals; white-collar criminals; and petty, habitual, unskilled, and frequently incarcerated offenders. (1) The professional criminal organizes his life around criminal activities from which he receives a primary source of income. (2) He lives and "plays out" the criminal role, an important basis for his personal identity, along with other roles (e.g., a lover) in communities where hustling and straight world roles intersect, contest, supplement, and support one another. He "fits in" and maintains social relationships in this community where he has the reputation among some of being a professional criminal. (3) He possesses some criminal skills, is at least moderately financially successful from criminal pursuits, and avoids frequent incarcerations in correctional institutions and associations with habitual petty offenders. (4) He is not merely a career criminal but a professional with a career in crime. It follows from this construction that professional crime encompasses the criminal's milieu: interactional behavior settings; identifiable work and play activities; career contigencies; and the related roles of criminal co-workers, victims, and supporting actors—that is, tipsters, fences, bail bondsmen, attorneys, confidants, and the police.

SELECTED LITERATURE REVIEW

Classical Theorists

The sociological analysis of professional crime begins with Sutherland's writings in the 1930s and 1940s (Sutherland, 1937; Sutherland and Cressey, 1970). He attempted to order the wide range of heterogeneous criminal behaviors into homogeneous units—that is, "behavior systems" (corresponding to the current sociological constructs "subculture" and "reference groups"). The behavior system contains a unit of acts and actors making up a group way of life, shared patterned behavior, and feelings of group identification. Sutherland's focus on criminal behavior systems, rather than individual criminals, enabled him and his followers to isolate and analyze various types of criminal behavior (Sutherland and Cressey, 1970: 238-239; Walker, 1981). He first analyzed professional theft as a behavior system. Professional thieves must have been tutored by professional thieves and must have been recognized as professional thieves by other professional thieves.

Five essential elements characterize Sutherland's behavior system: (1) technical skills (planning, technique, specialization): (2) status, involving respect from other professional thieves based on the accumulation of money, and respect from employees in the administration of criminal justice, politicians, and the media (status embracing the thief's sense of obligation to the profession and pride in group membership); (3) consensus, designating a shared ideology including a code of conduct (e.g., "Thou shall not squeal"), esprit de corps, collective self-protection, emotional support, and "we" feelings; (4) differential association or "hanging together" as a social unit, working together, avoiding friendly relationships with straight people, and congregating in criminal hangouts for purposes of camaraderie and the discussion of exploits and future ventures; and (5) organization, constituting the ordered activities of the mob (that is, three or four persons enjoined to plan and execute a series of thefts). Mobs, though variable in longevity and criminal activities, negotiate with a number of legitimate and illegitimate actors, such as "fixers" who bribe police, victims, prosecutors or judges to keep the thief out of jail. Mobs, in their patterned activities, pass on a subculture of professional theft.

Maurer (1940, 1964), writing in the 1940s and 1950s, defined the professional criminal in similar fashion to Sutherland. The professional criminal identifies with one or several underworld clusters or subcultures" formulated and recognized as such by criminals themselves: (1) the heavy rackets, peopled by criminals utilizing violence; (2) grift crimes composed of those who utilize skill and wit; (3) lone wolf criminals; and (4) quasi-criminals, including prostitutes and narcotic addicts. Professionals are located on a status continuum specific to the particular racket. The working unit of the professional criminal is the mob.

Sutherland's behavior system theory of professional crime remained unchallenged from the early 1950s through the middle 1960s among sociological criminologists, though several criminal typologists during this period following the seminal lead of Lindesmith and Dunham (1941), who verified and analyzed several additional criminal types, such as professional heavies, carnival drifters, political criminals, organized criminals, occupational criminals, auto thieves, extortionists, short con men, jack-of-all-trades offenders, gamblers, prostitutes, shoplifters, narcotic offenders, and fraud and forgery offenders (Cavan, 1962: 92-220; Cameron, 1964; Clinard and Quinney, 1967; Gibbons, 1977: 239-301; Roebuck, 1967; Roebuck and Frese, 1976; Roebuck and Weeber, 1978).

Lemert (1958) published a paper in 1958 on systematic check forgers based on an incarcerated sample. Though he did not equate his check writers with Sutherland's professional thieves, he compared the two and showed his subjects to be isolated criminals who avoided cooperative crime and any other association with criminals. Further, these forgers worked without highly technical skills and the advantage of the "fix." Lemert maintained that the nature of check writing and check usage has changed over time (e.g., introduction of check-writing machines and the increased use of payroll checks), thus reducing the success of forgery gangs while increasing lone check forgers. To some criminologists, the dearth of a criminal behavior system among check career criminals challenged Sutherland's thesis (Walker, 1981).

Contemporary Theorists and Findings

A new era in the study and conceptualization of professional crime began in 1966 under the aegis of the President's Commission on Law Enforcement and the Administration of Justice, when a group of sociologists headed by Leroy Gould (1966) embarked on an investigation of professional crime. This group began with a new and elastic definition of professional criminals—"individuals whose major source of income is from criminal pursuits and who spend a majority of their working time in illegal enterprises, (excluding) regular members of crime syndicates or people who engage in illegal activities as part of an otherwise legal profession" (Gould et al., 1966: 10). Thus, professional crime to the Gould group becomes an occupation, and the stress is more on income rather than skilled techniques or organization.

The data gathered on criminals and their crimes from law enforcement agencies in several cities and from interviews with a large number of criminals in jail and on the street disclosed a wide variety of criminal activities (auto theft, theft, burglary, fraud, illegal abortion, credit card theft, arson, murder, cartage theft, check forgery). These crimes were engaged in fairly indiscriminately by a wide assortment of offenders who differed in technical skills, wealth, and lifestyles. Criminal activities centered on the "hustle" rather than the mob. "To hustle is to be persistently on the lookout for an opportunity to make an illegal buck. A criminal 'on the hustle' will do pretty much whatever is required; he will consider whatever comes up" (Gould, 1966: 25). Success at hustling, therefore, requires an active, open attitude toward tackling a wide assortment of criminal activities and targets (Walker, 1981). Gould's group found that criminal activities were organized around the job at hand rather than any mob and that criminal associations in the main were of short duration. When the criminal job was completed criminal groups disbanded, though at times they might reassemble for another criminal undertaking. Stable relationships were sometimes detected among a few very successful criminals, but stable mobs were rare. Consensus and specialized skill in the Sutherland sense were not in evidence, and even "ratting" to the police was not uncommon. Almost all the criminals studied had a preferred line, but the opportunity structure of crime required versatility.

Obviously, Sutherland's behavior system thesis is not applicable to an explication of Gould's criminals; but unlike Sutherland, he dealt with a heterogeneous group of street criminals, many of whom were unsuccessful by any standards. Gould's subjects did maintain moderately stable relationships with several legitimate figures whose roles were supportive and complementary to the thief's way of life. For example, the fence buys stolen property and often encourages and abets the thief in his selection of goods to steal and targets the hit. The "juice man" (loan shark) lends the thief expense money between jobs, "up-front" money for the planning and execution of criminal jobs (e.g., the renting of vehicles) and money when arrested for the bail bondsmen and an attorney. Frequently, after release on bail the thief must resort to risky criminal activities to pay the bondsman and the lawyer. If he is rearrested, the bail is higher and the lawyer must continue to be paid. Negotiations involving appeals, case continuances, bonds, and plea bargaining require continuing criminal pursuits to finance increased further payments to the juice man, the bondsman, and the lawyer (Plate, 1975).

The Gould group also examined the relationships between career crime and law enforcement systems and revealed that the structure of crime includes routine functions of the law enforcement and criminal court systems that often sustain the offender. Specialized squads (homicide, burglary, vice, etc.) were assigned individual cases, though any one criminal could, within any given time, commit a variety of crimes and thereby come to the attention of several police units— units that might be unaware that other units were on the case. Sometimes a dearth of communication and shared information between police detective squads precluded arrest, investigation, and/or conviction. Unlike Sutherland and Maurer, Gould found no evidence of a systematic fix. Often, the busy and overloaded district attorney compromised with the offender via his attorney in a process of plea bargaining resulting in fines rather than incarcerations, or lighter sentences in lieu of felony time. Sometimes district attorneys declined to prosecute should an uncooperating victim prefer compensation from the perpetrator rather than prosecution. The courts often released the offender on high bond, cooperated with the prosecutor via the plea-bargaining process, and granted case continuances and appeals—all of which abetted the criminal's subversion of or adaptation to the administration of criminal justice, thereby sustaining a criminal career.

In summary, Gould's group brought into question Sutherland and Maurer's cohesive behavior systems. Their expanded definition of professional crime to include career crime permitted the delineation and empirical study of a much larger sample of criminals (and their tie-ins with other work roles) than those previously analyzed by traditional criminologists. However, because of their elastic definition and amorphous samples, it is unlikely that many real professional criminals were studied.

Since the 1960s a number of criminologists have registered the decline in the number of professional thieves as defined by Sutherland (Inciardi, 1975). Messinger (1966) holds, on the basis of interviews with criminals and law enforcment officials in a western U.S. city, that the "old-time professionals are a dying breed," and that pride in work is passing from both the noncriminal and criminal world. He proclaims the passing of the specialist, the disappearance of the expert and the tutelage system, and the weakening of loyalty among criminals. He observed that much criminal activity appeared to be a form of moonlighting in support of legitimate but low-paying jobs. Hustling for "anything that's up" was the name of the game. Messinger, like Inciardi, claims that changing social conditions have modified the nature of professional crime—for example, as checks and credit cards replace cash and improvement in the design of safes and burglar alarms increase, safes become increasingly undesirable targets. To Messinger the decline of Sutherland's thieves is not because of a decrease in the number of persons with talent for or an interest in crime as a living, but because of an increase in the range of quasi-legal economic enterprises that attract skillful potential criminals, such as consumer manipulation schemes through the "hard sell," the used car businesses, contracting, real estates sales, the repair business, and health studios. Messinger found it difficult to distinguish between criminal and legitimate enterprises; for example, many legitimate jewelers and retail store owners fence stolen property. He postulated a latent labor force of criminals waiting around for criminal or quasi-criminal jobs. Finally, he identified a few professional criminals defined as follows: Their activities were pursued for income with which to live; they had a main line of criminal work despite their versatility; they used some argot terms; they knew and practiced some elements of a criminal code; and they felt little if any guilt or shame about committing crime (Messinger, 1966). Unfortunately, Messinger's sample, like Gould's, did not include many real professional criminals, but rather a group of losers at crime.

From the late 1960s through the 1970s researchers tended to adopt either a more economic approach or a sociology of work frame of reference to the study of professional crime (Walker, 1981). In many studies these two perspectives are mixed, perforce.

Letkemann (1973) analyzed the behavioral dimensions of professional crime as an occupation via informal discussions and interviews with several paroled habitual offenders (key informants) and 45 Canadian federal prisoners. The latter were professional thieves known to have a preferred line of criminal activity. All identified themselves as "rounders" or "true criminals" (thoroughly committed to crime and an illegitimate lifestyle). They reported honesty and reliability in their dealings with co-workers and accomplices. All were highly skilled and took pride in their work. The criminal line comprised a generalized work preference and a related repertoire of skills adaptable to various related property crimes. Though necessarily versatile because of variable and problematic criminal opportunities, they carefully planned each criminal job. Rounders reported enduring connections and relationships throughout a criminal subculture; however, they did not work in mobs, but rather in transitory work crews with trusted colleagues. Self-defined elitists, they made clear-cut distinctions between themselves and "amateurs," "young punks," "dope fiends," and "alkies." All had business connections with fences.

Rounders shared a lifestyle with a peer group that offered them social acceptance, camaraderie, and criminal information (e.g., what fence is in need of what, what parts of the city are hot). They, like many legitimate people, had made a rational career choice, a career in crime with some knowledge of the vicissitudes entailed. Letkemann examined the technical dimensions of burglary, safecracking and robbery as practiced by his subjects and detected three classes of criminal skills: mechanical skills including tools and procedures; organizational skills comprising group leadership, planning, and execution; and social skills involving victim management and the control of tension.

All of Letkemann's subjects began their criminal careers during adolescence, and early delinquency was a prerequisite to adult criminal careers. Delinquency provided an education in the illegitimate lifestyle, including rudimentary criminal skills, criminal role models, and a reformatory experience, which opened the door for associations with criminals. Prison experience taught them the value of friendships and provided connections with career criminals. Technical skills for later criminal jobs were learned from criminal companions and through trades-training prison assignments (e.g., building trades). The aspirant rounder needed social skills and connections necessary to the establishment of friendships with rounders in order to work with and learn from experienced criminals. Most rounders grew up with friends and relatives who "took them on" or arranged for others to take them. Likable novices made friends with rounders in thief bars, hotels, and hangouts and learned by doing (Letkemann, 1973: 117-136).

Letkemann demonstrated with a sample of "professional" criminals that a criminal career is a type of work or occupation involving skills, tools, and a time dimension. An explicit, conscious commitment to criminal activity as a means of making some portion of one's livelihood was found to be the most useful criterion in differentiating professional and nonprofessional offenders. He demonstrated that a criminal career could be analyzed in similar fashion to a legitimate career.

Letkemann's chief and probably unintended contribution was the finding that professional thieves and professional theft are not as amorphous and unidentifiable as Gould and his followers have claimed. His criminals did not belong to semipermanent mobs, nor did they meet totally all of Sutherland's behavior system requirements. However, they did approximate Sutherland's professional thieves along several significant dimensions. Unlike Gould's and Messinger's offenders, many of whom were petty, habitual offenders, Letkemann's subjects were true professionals—and *therein lies the difference in the findings.* A similar study to Letkemann's utilizing unincarcerated professional criminals would probably disclose a group of professional thieves even closer to Sutherland's model. At least one study suggests that this is the case (Roebuck and Frese, 1976).

Miller (1978: 23-55), utilizing a series of empirical studies by criminologists in the late 1960s and the 1970s, treated deviant work including career crime as a type of social organization. He analyzed, among other deviant types, the patterned and identifiable work activities, roles, relationships, values, and work rationales of career criminals involved in armed robbery, burglary, safecracking, confidence operations, medical quackery and fortunetelling. Career burglars and robbers lived in a world or "social niche" occupied by a variety of actors engaged in diverse skills and activities, and were linked via supportive and complementary roles—for example, victims, tipsters (suppliers of information to thieves about victims and targets), fences, bail bondsmen, and attorneys. The relationships characterizing their world were of the exchange type, those of the marketplace. Career thieves rationalized away their work as no more dishonest than others—others are either better able to hide dishonest activities or they have the power to impose their conceptions and activities on others.

Miller's burglars and robbers had some characteristics of Sutherland's professional thieves. Many were skilled criminals who approached work with some degree of pride, discipline, and rationality. Many worked within groups similar to Sutherland's mobs and enjoyed peer group prestige based on material accumulation. The "pure fix" was not found, though plea bargaining and other indirect tactics to beat the criminal justice system similar to those found by Gould were reported. Few shared an ideology as developed or binding as that described by Sutherland. Rules and values that influenced behavior were short term, job-specific, and limited to the current work group.

Confidence operators, medical quacks, and fortunetellers, those with false pretense work roles, depended on social skills enabling them to manipulate people and settings. The nature of such deviant work encouraged a degree of isolation and individualism that was not conducive to the development of a professional-thief mob or culture. Work rationalizations included the dictum that everyone is dishonest, though some medical quacks and fortunetellers claimed to perform valuable services.

Miller claims that because of the flexible and variable organization of most forms of deviant work, definitive career patterns are hard to delineate for any one type career. The immediate opportunity structure available in conjunction with the worker's skills, contacts, and personal preferences was found to bę most important in deviant career entry. Miller's deviant career contingency views are summarized as follows: (1) Deviant workers gradually drift into deviant work as a consequence of regular activities within or without the career line—those without are similar to those within. (2) Many acquire the needed skills by a combination of informal training by other deviant workers and on-the-job learning. (3) Many enter a deviant field to make more money than they could make in legitimate employment. (4) Many are initially employed in the entertainment-restaurant-liquor industry where skills and rationales are learned necessary to deviant work roles. (5) Many grow up in neighborhoods where the availability of deviant career opportunities is always present. Miller's "social niche" replaces Sutherland's mob, and his findings are similar to Letkemann's.

Some of the most significant data on professional criminals have been gathered by Pruis and Irini (1980) in an ethnographic study of the social organization of a quasi-slum hotel community located in a northeastern city. They focused on the interrelatedness of the social and career roles found among a group of people who lived and worked in an "underside" community that catered to the sensual and illicit entertainment needs of insiders and outsiders, to the work needs of insiders engaged in a variety of quasi-legal and illegal hustles (bartenders, waiters, waitresses, hookers, criminals, desk clerks, strippers), and to an assortment of night people either employed in or patrons of the bar-restaurant-hotel business. Many insiders had been arrested, some incarcerated; some were into drugs and gambling; and many dealt with loan sharks. The methodology encompassed participant observation, socializing with the actors in various social contexts; work observations (desk clerk, waiter, bartender); and lengthy personal interviews with an assortment of deviant actors.

They found a number of "rounders" or "true criminals" (subject designations) who were engaged in a variety of professional career crime activities comprising both heavy and false pretense offenses. These "good hustlers" were knowledgeable about street life, capable, connected with other rounders, solid (trustworthy), "honest" (with crime partners), committed to crime, heavily into criminal action, and free of organizational ties.

Rounders started out as "fringe rounders" (a less skilled group who hustled for lesser scores, worked with less experienced criminals, and were arrested more frequently) and had worked their way up to rounder status through and by criminal skill, dedication to career theft, coolness under pressure, guts, larceny sense, likability, conning ability, reputation as a "solid guy," and contacts with and acceptance by rounders. Most fringe rounders never made it. Most rounders grew up "in the life," experienced trouble with the police earlier on, and frequently did time as juveniles and young adults. While fringe rounders, they moonlighted at bar-restaurant-hotel work always linked to some kind of hustle. For example, as waiters or bartenders they simultaneously peddled drugs and stolen property, or worked as loan sharks. Most, while fringe rounders, were sponsored by relatives and friends, who found them work and introduced them to rounders. Sponsors were either rounders themselves or solid employers, or employees in the hotel community.

The rounder's life was organized around several themes: street wisdom, hustling skills, contacts, reputations, mobility, and action. Street wisdom is knowing where the illegal action is happening; knowing about after-hours clubs, gambling games, drug deals, thieves, strippers and hookers; police activities; fencing operations; and knowing who to tell what, where, and when. Rounders hustle everyone but a thief; he or she might hustle other thieves if not a current partner in crime. They trust only co-workers on a particular job and only help (warn about the police and working hazards, pay bond for, lend money to) fellow thieves. There is some honesty among thieves. Threats to kill dishonest co-workers are infrequently carried out, though they tend to "slander" the offender, thereby discouraging other thieves from working with him. Hustling attributes are generalizable across situations, and diversity may promote one's longevity in a hustling career. Contacts and personal relationships must be negotiated and maintained with other rounders and people in the hotel community. There is no successful hustling without contacts, and those who hustle at a particular job alone are often facilitated by the efforts of a partner, a tipster, or a fence. Futhermore, good thieves must have help in processing their goods. Some hustlers "finger," work out plans, and secure burglary crews for criminal jobs without direct personal participation. Reputation is based on one's capabilities, connections, coolness under pressure, guts, personal integrity, and solidity.

Rounders participated in sociability action involvements, comprising a nexus of blowing money on women, gambling, booze, and "being somebody." Most rounders hustled in or nearby the community where they grew up because that was the territory they knew and where they had connections.

Female rounders were similar to their male counterparts, though in most cases not as thoroughly professionalized. Many drifted into career theft as a sideline to work activities as waitresses, bar maids, strippers, exotic dancers, and/or hookers (prostitutes). Hookers simultaneously worked at picking pockets, boosting (shoplifting), and fencing. Other female rounders were involved in theft, drug dealing, and fencing. Like male rounding, female hustling involvement varied over a period of time. A girl might be engaged primarily in boosting one season and then move over into hooking or drug dealing the next, or she might be heavily engaged in all three over the same period of time. Female rounders engaged in friendly and sexual relationships with all types of working men in the hotel community without incurring jealousy. They preferred male rounders. Few had families of their own and played the field just like male rounders.

Though several social types were described, emphasis was directed to the interrelatedness and overlapping of community roles. Rounders were involved through friendship, marriage, family, or work ties with others who were engaged in a wide variety of illegal and legal pursuits. A female might be a waitress, hooker, stripper, fence, or a drug dealer on either a sequential or overlapping basis. The same female might be dating a bar or hotel manager, and her brother might be a rounder. Community members played several roles over time and several roles at the same time. Overall reputation depended on an individual's contacts and his recognition as being solid as well as particular role involvements.

The rounders' and other actors' career contingencies inhered in multiple routings: (1) closing, through necessity, on what was in keeping with skills, contacts, work preferences, and opportunities; (2) recruitment, by (a) inadvertent involvement (being at the right place at the right time for work), (b) sponsored involvements (set up by insiders), and (c) solicited involvements (insiders seek you out); (3) drift, resulting from available alternatives free from moral restraint; (4) conversion or commitment to the hustlers' way of life. One gradually becomes a thief. The designation thief might reflect one's present activities, albeit with the now explicit recognition that one is, for example, a thief. One must become tolerant or accepting of all activities comprising the lifestyle of a thief and realize that by wider community standards he is disrespectable. Other elements are (5) continuance commitments resulting from the realization that one was unable to make as much money in legitimate work as at theft; that one's lifestyle required more money than legitimate employment would pay for; that widespread hustling opportunities were available; and that legitimate work was not available for him. Friendships, work ties, and emotional and financial dependencies on people in the life also precluded disinvolvement—embeddedness in the social life of the hotel community; (6) reputation and identities referring to the general rule that the sooner, and more totally, persons accept identities in the hustling world, the more likely they were to continue in their illegal pursuits. *Being somebody that is solid is difficult if not impossible to transfer to a conventional world role*; and (7) disinvolvement among rounders, which was infrequent. They became accustomed to "being their own boss," and they disliked routine legitimate employment. Unsteady and sketchy legitimate work records precluded the entrance of many into the straight world. The fear of or an actual arrest and conviction retired some. Infirmities resulting from age or booze incapacitated others. A few obtained jobs in or bought into quasi-legal businesses (e.g., bars, restaurants, hotels—usually in the hotel community) which precluded a total commitment to the life; but even these few continued hustling as a part of, or a sideline to, the so-called legitimate enterprise. Some died of natural causes; some were killed. Most never left the life completely, though many became downwardly mobile, ending up as street drunks and bums or petty, habitual criminals. Still a few others were reduced in status to fringe rounders.

Pruis and Irini, though greatly indebted to Letkemann, have made several major contributions. First, they demonstrated, as did Letkemann, that professional criminals similar to Sutherland's professional thieves (on several dimensions) are on the scene and viable. The rounder fits into a *community criminal behavior system rather than a criminal-mob-behavior system.* Consensus and specialization in this system are not as marked as in Sutherland's, but they are present to some degree within a larger system. They, like Sutherland and Letkemann, utilized an interactionist approach; and their thieves (the actors themselves), like Sutherland's, described and verified a criminal behavior system of which they were a part. Neither Sutherland nor Pruis and Irini constructed such a system a priori. Pruis and Irini's analysis of the interrelatedness of a quasi-hustling and hustling community has no peer in the literature. Moreover, they validate for the first time a set of specific criminal career contingencies that are anchored in and supported by empirical data. Further, like Gould and Messinger, they tie in crime with the wider social organization.

CONCLUSION

The foregoing literature review confirms that to date there is no full agreement among criminologists about the definition of professional criminals or professional crime. Researchers and scholars vary in approach, semantics, conceptualizations, and methodologies. Therefore, their findings are divergent. The heterogeneity of criminal subjects that make up sample studies is the major research problem. Despite their differences in approach or findings, however, few if any researchers would deny the existence of career criminals who approximate the professional criminal. The degree of the approximation is in question—that is, when or at what point does one have a criminal career? When or at what point does one's criminal career in crime become a profession? We propose two solutions to the problem. First, with reference to theory and method, we should return to a more elastic and extended version of Sutherland's behavior system approach as it has been modified by the criminal typologists (Gibbons, Clinard and Quinney, Roebuck) and criminal subculture researchers (Letkemann, Pruis and Irini). Such action would provide us with more homogeneous theoretical and constructed types and more uniform criminal samples and therefore, one can hope, more uniform results. Second, we should embark on an ongoing series of phenomenological studies of successful professional criminals in the open who have avoided frequent convictions and incarcerations. The implementation of both proposals would permit the study of truly professional criminals and simultaneously keep us abreast of the ever-shifting criminal scene that is anchored in the larger social system.

At the least we may conclude that the professional thief organizes his life around theft as a career and a source of self-esteem. He possesses some criminal skills, enjoys at least moderate financial success, and avoids frequent incarceration. Finally, he plays out the thief's role in communities where criminal and straight individuals contest as well as supplement and support one another. Urban criminal subcultures are maintained by belief and social systems that seem particularly durable and complex. Understanding and control depend on studying them in the natural settings in which they flourish. The emphasis of study must be on the professional thief's community niche and alignments rather than with Sutherland's outdated concept of the permanent criminal mob. Finally, the research data at hand enable us to understand why professional criminals persist in crime despite occasional arrests, convictions, and incarcerations. Vold (1958) anticipated as much, more than two decades ago.

REFERENCES

BARLOW, H. D. (1981) Introduction to Criminology. Boston: Little, Brown.

CAMERON, M. O. (1964) The Booster and the Snitch: Department Store Shoplifting. New York: Free Press.

CAVAN, R. S. (1962) Criminology. New York: Thomas Y. Crowell.

CLINARD, M. B. and R. QUINNEY (1967) Criminal Behavior Systems: A Typology. New York: Holt, Rinehart & Winston.

CONKLIN, J. E. (1981) Criminology. New York: Macmillan.

GIBBONS, D. C. (1977) Society, Crime, and Criminal Careers. Englewood Cliffs, NJ: Prentice-Hall.

GOULD, L. C. et al. (1966) Crime as a Profession. Washington, DC: Office of Law Enforcement Administration, Department of Justice.

INCIARDI, J. A. (1975) Careers in Crime. Chicago: Rand McNally.

IRWIN, J. (1970) The Felon. Englewood Cliffs, NJ: Prentice-Hall.

JACKSON, B. (1972) Outside the Law. New Brunswick, NJ: Transaction Books.

KLOCKARS, C. B. (1974) The Professional Fence. New York: Free Press.

LEMERT, E. M. (1958) "The behavior of the systematic check forger." Social Problems 6: 141-149.

LETKEMANN, P. (1973) Crime as Work. Englewood Cliffs, NJ: Prentice-Hall.

LINDESMITH, A. H. and H. W. DUNHAM (1941) "Some principals of criminal typology." Social Forces 29: 309-311.

MARTIN, J. B. (1952) My Life in Crime. Westport, CT: Greenwood.

MAURER, D. W. (1964) Whiz Mob: A Correlation of the Technical Argot of Pickpockets with their Behavior Pattern. New Haven, CT: College and University Press.

———(1940) The Big Con: A Story of the Confidence Man and the Confidence Game. Indianapolis: Bobb-Merrill.

MAYHEW, H. (1862) London's Underworld (P. Quennel, ed.). London: Spring Books.

MESSINGER, S. L. (1966) "Some reflections on 'professional crime' in West City." Mimeographed personal communication to authors.

MILLER, G. (1978) Odd Jobs: The World of Deviant Work. Englewood Cliffs, NJ: Prentice-Hall.

PLATE, T. (1975) Crime Pays! New York: Ballantine.

PRUIS, R. and S. IRINI (1980) Hookers, Rounders, and Desk Clerks: The Social Organization of the Hotel Community. Toronto: Gage Publishing.

QUINNEY, R. (1975) Criminology. Boston: Little, Brown.

RETTIG, R. et al. (1977) Manny: A Criminal Addict's Story. Boston: Houghton Mifflin.

ROEBUCK, J. B. (1967) Criminal Typology. Springfield, IL: Charles C Thomas.
———(1964) "The short con man." Crime and Deliquency 10: 235-248.
———and W. FRESE (1976) The Rendezvous: A Case Study of an After-Hours Club. New York: Free Press.
ROEBUCK, J. B. and S. WEEBER (1978) Political Crime in the United States. New York: Praeger.
SUTHERLAND, E. H. (1937) The Professional Thief. Chicago: University of Chicago Press.
———and D. R. CRESSEY (1970) Criminology, New York: J. P. Lippincott.
SYKES, G. M. (1956) Crime and Society. New York: Random House.
VOLD, G. B. (1958) Theoretical Criminology. New York: Oxford University Press.
VETTER, H. J.and I. J. SILVERMAN (1978) The Nature of Crime. Philadelphia: W. B. Saunders.
WALKER, A. (1981) "Sociology and professional crime," pp. 153-178 in A. S. Blumberg (ed.) Current Perspectives on Criminal Behavior. New York: Knopf.

James A. Inciardi

University of Delaware

2

ON GRIFT AT THE SUPERBOWL
Professional Pickpockets and the NFL

For centuries, pickpockets have congregated to work the crowds at sporting events. As early as the days of Shakespeare's youth, pickpocketing was a full-time profession common in London, Norwich, Exeter, and Bristol during the terms of court when thousands of countrymen were drawn to the cities for business and pleasure. The thieves frequented bowling alleys, dicing houses, and the resorts, assemblies, plays, and fairs where the unsuspecting visitor was easy prey (Judges, 1930; Aydelotte, 1913; Wheatley and Cunningham, 1891; Viles and Furnivall, 1880). In more recent times, the same phenomenon was apparent in New York, Chicago, Philadelphia, and other major American cities (Martin, 1868; Crapsey, 1872; Maurer, 1964). And the pattern of theft was identical. Pickpockets worked in mobs of two, three, or four members, each playing a specific role in the total operation. There was the selection of the "mark" (victim), the locating of the money or valuables on his person ("fanning"), maneuvering him into position, the act of theft, and the passing of the stolen property.

Although the literature over the years has referenced various types of pickpockets, ranging from the rank amateur to the seasoned expert, both history and folklore have described the pickpocket as a *professional thief* (Sutherland, 1937; Maurer, 1964; Inciardi, 1975). Along with a delimited number of sneak thieves, safe and house burglars, forgers and counterfeiters, shoplifters and confidence men, the seasoned pickpocket has been conceived of as a highly specialized, nonviolent criminal who makes a regular business of stealing. He devotes his entire working time and energy to larceny, operating with proficiency and possessing an extensive body of skills and knowledge that is utilized

31

in the planning and execution of his work. He is a graduate of a developmental process that includes the acquisition of specialized experience and attitudes. He makes crime his way of life, identifying himself with an underworld that extends friendship, understanding, sympathy, congeniality, security, recognition, and respect. Finally, he is able to steal for long periods without extended terms of incarceration as a result of his abilities in dealing with his victims and the various elements of social control.

The pickpocket, reflecting on this notion of professionalism, was known in the underworld as a "class cannon":

> class cannon means experience, skill, connections and a sense for knowing when to steal . . . it means that the *cannon* (picking pockets) is part of your life . . . it means that you're not one of those amateurs who spend their time *grinding up nickels and dimes* (inept stealing for low stakes).

METHOD

Ethnographic studies indicate that the class cannons described by Sutherland in 1937 and by Maurer years later continue to operate in many American cities. The data also show that every December, when thousands of tourists fill their wallets and fly to South Florida for a sunny vacation, along with them comes a small flock of professional pickpockets who consider the Miami area a pickpocket mecca.

My entree to the Miami pickpocket community occurred in 1972 (Inciardi, 1975, 1977). Through one informant known to me since 1966, introductions were made to a three-member pickpocket mob. These, in turn, arranged introductions to other grifters well known to them. Through this "snowball sampling" technique, repeated contacts have been made with these and other class cannons in numerous cities throughout the United States. The major difficulty with this technique involved locating pickpockets for lengthy interviews, including those with whom introductions had already been made. Like other members of the professional underworld, few seasoned pickpockets of the class cannon type have fixed abodes, mailing addresses, telephone numbers, or families or employers who know their whereabouts. The vast majority are wanderers, moving from city to city and from community to community, living along the fringes of society—in the skid rows and amusement centers, typically residing in the cheap hotels, flop houses, and anonymous rooming houses. As such, the sampling process also involved much waiting and watching at the race tracks, airports, carnivals, convention halls, arcades, and streets where the pickpockets generally worked. Upon observing one of those individual pickpockets previously introduced to the author, an approach would be made at a time when it was obvious that the thief was not "tracking a mark." Under these circumstances, a short conversation would often ensue with an arrangement for a later meeting at some other place.

Since 1972 on a sporadic and informal basis, both structured and unstructured interviews have been undertaken with a total of 42 class cannons. The majority of these took place in the Miami area during the winter months. However, interviews were also carried out in New York, Philadelphia, Salt Lake City, and San Francisco. During the course of these interviews, it was learned that in addition to their travels to South Florida, the Super Bowl every January was also a favorite workplace for class cannons (and other pickpockets as well). The commentary that follows is based on discussions with 11 of these expert thieves who have been traveling to the Super Bowl annually.

On the Grift at the Super Bowl

On Miami's Orange Bowl field, Pittsburgh Steelers quarterback Terry Bradshaw dropped back to survey the Dallas Cowboys' defensive line. In that instant, his eyes shifted to spot what he was looking for—an open receiver, more than half a field away. Bradshaw tightened his grip on the football, weighed it, aimed it, and sent it downwind.

In the stands, pickpocket Hester Mark leaned back to survey the Orange Bowl spectators. At that same instant, he, too, riveted his attention on a potential victim, just a few feet away. And just as Bradshaw, knowing precisely when to release his fingers to send the ball spiralling 64 yards down-field toward his receiver's hands, Hester Mark, knowing exactly how and when to flex his fingers, begin to draw a billfold from his victim's pants pocket. Terry Bradshaw set up a winning score, and so did Hester Mark. And later, just as the Dallas Cowboys, staggered by their 21-17 loss, were not quite sure of what had hit them, so was Hester Mark's victim of a loss over $200.

That was at Super Bowl X in Miami in 1976. In postgame reports, police and stadium officials noted that more than 60 wallets were reported stolen or found empty. Police estimated known cash losses to be some $6,000. That, however, was likely but a small portion of the actual losses. Hester Mark, with his two partners, lifted 30 wallets and left the stands with almost $2,000.

The situation was much the same during the Minnesota-Oakland confrontation in Pasadena at 1977's Super Bowl XI, at the Dallas-Denver game under the New Orleans Superdome in 1978, and at every Super Bowl since then.

According to the pickpocket informants, stealing at football games is nothing new. The annual journey of Miami's class cannons to Super Bowl city, however, at least for most of those interviewed, did not begin until 1977. According to Hester Mark:

> Sure, we know that there are dips (pickpockets) everywhere, and we know that from the day of the first football playoff game—wherever and whenever it was—the local amateurs and pros hit the stadiums . . . . But for most of us here, the idea of jacking across the country for one game didn't come up till a few years ago. Here we were down in the South hitting every Dolphins game at the Orange Bowl. The day's work was pretty good . . . $200-$400 a game. Then when the year's biggest sporting event came to town, we noticed a difference that day . . . a different kind of fan . . . richer, preoccupied, crazier, and a lot of pandemonium for 2-3 days.

Hester Mark went on to describe how, over the Super Bowl weekend, his mob's total thefts amounted to over $3,000.

Among the pickpockets who frequent the Super Bowl each year are perhaps some of the more colorful members of the professional underworld.

"Hester Mark" ("Hester" for Hester Street where he grew up and "Mark" for reasons known only to him)[2] was born on New York's Lower East Side shortly after the turn of the century and was 70 years old when last interviewed in 1980. The youngest son of Jewish immigrants, he learned his skills in 1929 from a barber on St. Mark's Place in New York's "West Village." He claims to have worked for Ringling Brothers and was once a short-change artist on Coney Island. In the 1930s he followed circuses and carnivals as a con artist and pickpocket. Hester Mark could have been created by the late American journalist and author Damon Runyon, who peopled his stories with such Broadway characters as the Lemon Drop Kid and Harry the Horse. When Hester Mark speaks, he talks from the side of his mouth, and he prefaces almost every sentence with "Listen" or "Sure." He always wears a hat, and he always carries a newspaper—used presumably to conceal the movement of his hand. In a career that spans a half-century,

Hester Mark has been arrested more than 100 times, at least 60 of these for picking pockets, and he has never been convicted of a felony.

"Happy Louis" (or Louie the Painter), age 72 in 1982, has been picking pockets for 41 years and is a high school graduate who also attended law school in Chicago for two years. He learned to pick pockets as a bartender in Boston from a waterfront burglar known as Eddie Pear, a childhood friend from Portland, Maine. Of his estimated 52 arrests, all but five were for pickpocketing, and he has served a total of ten years in prison.

"Hymie John," the son of German immigrants, was born on New York's Lower East Side in 1900. When last contacted in 1979, he had been a pickpocket for 53 years. Nearly bald, with heavy sideburns, John speaks rapidly and spits regularly. He tells that he learned to pick pockets by a remnant of the Old Border Gang, a notorious troupe of thieves from turn-of-the-century New York. His schooling in theft took place in the back of a candy store in Hester Street. Of his 66 arrests, 40 have been for picking pockets; his first was when he was age 12 for being an accomplice in a bank robbery. He once recalled that the robbery was planned for New Year's Eve in 1913 in Southhampton on Long Island. As a child, his role was simple: He was to crawl through a small window and open the front door for his fellow thieves, who would then rob the safe. But he couldn't unlock the door. The police were called, his friends departed on horseback, leaving him inside, where the police quickly found him. John has spent a total of 13 years in jails and prisons and says he has nine escapes on his record.

"Bat Masterson" does not carry the bat (or cane) that was the trademark of the man whose relative he claims to be and whose name he adopted: William Barclay Masterson, friend of Wyatt Earp and later U.S. Marshall for New York State's Southern District. Masterson, age 51 in 1976 and born in San Francisco, worked as a waiter in New York's Stork Club and as a busboy in some of midtown Manhattan's more elegant restaurants. At 25, he killed a man in a bar fight on New York City's Eighth Avenue. He was convicted of manslaughter and served eight years of his sentence, mostly in New York's Sing Sing and Green Haven prisons. He learned to pick pockets while in prison. Although he wasn't paroled until 1959, he has considered the cannon his trade since 1956 because of thefts he committed behind bars. He has been arrested ten other times, all for pickpocketing.

"Fred Hein," also known as Freddie the Hat, Deutsche Fred, and Fritz the German, was 67 in 1982. He has been a pickpocket for 35 years, ever since his New York bakery failed. He learned his second trade while working at his first, from a cannon and short-change artist who was one of his employees. Fred is a small man, just over five feet tall, with extremely large hands; he often wears an oversized broad-brimmed hat with an orange fishing lure tucked in its band, along with a cheap pin-striped suit several sizes too big. One would expect that his stature and zoot suit attire would draw attention to him—the last thing that any good cannon would wish. But "on workdays" he stated, "I get rid of my theatrical costume and dress like the rest of the tourists and sportsfans . . . . I only wear the costume for laughs, sometimes, when I'm living down here on this geriatric skid row (south Miami Beach)."

"Crying Phil," the initial and most regular of my informants, has been a pickpocket and thief most of his life. Born in Brooklyn, New York and of Jewish parentage, Phil retired from picking pockets in 1980 at the age of 69. His career spans more than half a century, and he claims to have practiced his craft from Chicago to Capetown and from Houston to Hong Kong. Having survived more than 100 arrests in his lifetime, he now lives comfortably in a small Miami Beach con-dominium, left to him by his parents. He last visited the Super Bowl in 1979, but he does keep in touch with his pickpocket associates. Phil was forced out of his profession by arthritis.

All of the pickpockets interviewed seemed to agree that the Super Bowl provides an unusually good opportunity to steal. First, the fans who journey to the Super Bowl come from all over the country expec-ting to have an explosive weekend. They bring large amounts of cash and take few precautions for protecting it. Second, the game is always held in a warm climate or in a temperature-controlled indoor stadium. Thus, the pickpocket rarely has a victim's outer clothing to deal with. Third, with the betting that goes on in the stands combined with repeated purchases of food, drinks, and souvenirs, fans are always reaching for their wallets. This tells the pickpocket where the victim's money is kept and eliminates the need for "fanning the mark" (feeling the victim's outer clothing to locate the billfold). Fourth, the excite-ment of the game keeps the fans' attention on the ball field. Little thought is given to the people around them, especially to the possibility of pickpockets. Fifth, there are other distractions as well. At Super Bowl X in Miami's Orange Bowl in 1976, before the game as thousands queued to get in, there were arguments and shouts of dismay at the discovery of forgotten or suddenly missing tickets, tickets held for nonexistent seats, or tickets scalped at outrageous prices.

Inside, there were spectacles other than the one on the field. There were celebrities and near-celebrities to watch: Joe DiMaggio, Raquel Welch, Andy Williams, Ethel Kennedy, O.J. Simpson. There were aerial acts, of a sort, to view: helicopters ferrying passengers to the field, small planes towing advertising banners, and of course, the Goodyear blimp. There were filmmakers at the game shooting footage for *Black Sunday*, a disaster movie about a fictitious Super Bowl game played at the Orange Bowl. And there was the exotic dancer from Atlanta who ran onto the field during the fourth quarter of the game to present a good luck token to a rather bemused Dallas Cowboy. Sixth, the Super Bowl stadium is always overcrowded; there are long lines at the concession stands and crowded aisles, giving the pickpocket added cover in which to work. At Super Bowl XIV in the Rose Bowl on January 20, 1980, for example, 103,985 ticketed fans crammed into the stadium. And seventh, the opportunities for picking pockets do not end with the final gun signaling the end of the game. Tens of thousands of fans mill around the stadium, often for hours after the close of the game; there are throngs crowding the aisles, exit ramps, and parking lots; and there are the Super Bowl parties in jam-packed bars both before and after the game.

Each pickpocket, or mob, seems to have its own special technique for working a Super Bowl game. One cannon noted that he picks out a group of fans and sets to work when their team has possession of the ball. Another moves in for a take only when the quarterback throws a long pass—a time when most fans jump to their feet. Still a third does most of his work when there are injuries on the field, since many potential victims take that opportunity to mill around or head up the aisles to the restroooms or concession stands. Others spread their activities to the concessions and the bathroom entrances.

Of the pickpockets interviewed, Hymie John, operating alone at Super Bowl XIV in Pasadena, seemed to have the most unique style. He wandered throughout the Rose Bowl, never watching the game, but listening to it on an AM radio headset. He always watched the crowd and listened to the plays so as to anticipate the time to make his move. He recalled:

> I made my first score midway in the first quarter when Bradshaw threw his first bomb to Swann. Almost seconds later I hit again when Bahr kicked the 21-yard field goal for the Steelers . . . . My best scores were during Franco Harris's touchdown run in the second quarter and Swann's

47-yard catch from Bradshaw early in the third . . . . I remember those especially, I'll never forget them, 'cause between the two I walked away with almost $900.

On an alternative point, while most of the pickpockets interviewed feel comfortable working at any Super Bowl site, others do have their preferences. On the Rose Bowl, one class cannon stated in 1982, "the place is a damn antique, can't move around, aisles are too tight . . . can't make a fast break if you're pushed to." Yet a member of the same mob countered:

Wrong-o . . . . you work the opportunity the place gives you. Sure the Rose is an old-time dump . . . but look at those end zones. The seats are only 17 inches wide, everyone is climbin' on top of each other, and its dark back there . . . it's always in the shade.

On the New Orleans Superdome, Bat Masterson commented: "I prefer these modern stadiums. Lots of room to work." And on the Miami Orange Bowl, Crying Phil recalled:

The place has so few bathrooms that the lineup can be a mile long. You'll see a guy down near the end of the line that's got to go so bad that he's bent over with his nuts in his hand. You just cut through the line behind him, excuse yourself, and take his money as you pass.

The Passing of the Class Cannon

Despite the presence of the class cannons at the Super Bowl each year and their winter congregations in Miami, evidence has suggested that these expert pickpockets have all but disappeared. Maurer (1964: 171) estimated that in 1945 there were some 5,000-6,000 class cannons operating in the United States, with a reduction to about 1,000 by 1955. By 1965, according to one expert cannon from New York City's Times Square area, the total number suffered even further reduction:

Most of the ones left are old timers, and I say that there are probably no more than six or seven hundred in the whole country, if that much. There are plenty of amateurs, young ones, prostitutes, addicts, but they were never associated with the old-time mobs [Inciardi, 1975: 21].

Similarly, an officer from the Pickpocket and Confidence Squad of the New York City Police Department indicated in 1966:

You see very few of the real experts these days. They have either quit, died, or are in jail, and they are rarely replaced. Most of the newer boys are from Harlem, and you can spot them a block away [Inciardi, 1975: 21].

In January 1974, a 72-year-old retired pickpocket working as a part-time clerk in a Miami Beach retirement hotel observed:

Gone forever are the times of the pants pocket *gonnif*. I've seen less and less of them since the start of the 1950's . . . . An estimate? Who knows . . . . When I packed it in four years ago we had maybe six hundred. Now . . . probably less, I'm sure [Inciardi, 1977: 61].

In 1976, a 62-year-old cannon operating in downtown Miami stated:

Each year you'll see about fifty of us pass through Miami; . . . it's a tradition. You go up to New York and Philly in the summer, and to Chicago in the fall, and you see the same guys most of the time . . . I'd say if you put all of us together you couldn't fill an old-time nickelodeon . . . maybe three hundred, maybe four [Inciardi, 1977: 62].

And most recently, in 1982, Crying Phil commented:

There's just a handful of the experts left. Most of what you see now are bums, amateurs and Colombians . . . the Colombian dips are what you see most . . . but they have no class.

The decline of the class cannon has seemingly been the result of a process that began as far distant as the turn of the twentieth century. The pickpocket, as part of the professional underworld, has enjoyed the security of a criminal lifestyle that was for the most part immune from the forces of social control. This immunity perpetuated contact among members of the profession, permitting the development of a subculture aimed at maintaining a low level of social visibility. An intricate network of relationships and argot developed for the purpose of keeping out "outsiders'—amateur criminals—and a code of ethics was constructed for internal social control. Dissemination of information regarding case fixing and untrustworthy members of the profession developed to maintain a defense system against the infiltration of any representative of the wider social world. As such, this specialized segment of the underworld operated within a "functional superstructure" of isolation, protection, and group support (Inciardi, 1975: 75-82).

The process that caused the decline of professional pickpockets was one that served to erode the foundations of this superstructure. Since the turn of the century, the increased cooperative relationships between local, state, and federal law enforcement groups, as well as growth in the technology of communication systems, combined to impinge on the almost unlimited security that had been enjoyed by interstate fugitives. Fingerprinting, begun in this country in 1903, rapidly emerged as an infallible means of personal identification. Federal legislation relative to interstate flight and the various habitual offender laws served to create preliminary obstacles to case fixing, and the bureaucratization of many police agencies and court systems made the fixing of cases even more difficult.

The convergence of these and other factors not only reduced the number of active professional pickpockets but, in doing so, also weakened the stability of the profession as a long-term economic pursuit, thus creating significant shortages in the number of potential recruits. With only a few new recruits to a career that was rapidly becoming more visible, the subculture began to atrophy, leaving behind only the seasoned old-timers who had no other profession to turn to yet had enough accumulated experience to survive. In this behalf, one hanger-on to the profession stated in 1972:

> Tougher and tougher things have been getting lately. It's still easy to steal, but it's the *fixing* that's tougher. You can't do it as often as before, and if you can, it costs a fortune . . . . Things just aren't that profitable no more and the newcomers realize it [Inciardi, 1977: 63].

Thus, given this process, it is likely that the cannon will continue to atrophy until its more unique qualities become only brief references within the history of crime. In this behalf, Crying Phil summed it up quite well:

> There will never be another cannon like Eddie the Immune, a Chicago pickpocket from 1890 to the 1930s. Eddie was arrested hundreds of times . . . . He fixed so many of his arrests that he spent only ten days in jail . . . I'm told he died a rich man.

NOTES

1. This quotation was drawn from Inciardi (1977), who provides a more complete description of the class cannon.

2. Most pickpockets are known by their underworld nicknames, or "monikers." The majority of professional thieves, and some other criminals as well, abandon their family names and assume others that remain with them in the underworld throughout their lives. The moniker is usually a colorful designation, and, reflecting the practice of primitive peoples, its acquisition may represent a commemoration of some personal characteristic, exploit, or former occupation, or it may designate a professional thief's place of birth or some other location pertinent to his life history (see Inciardi, 1975: 57).

REFERENCES

AYDELOTTE, F. (1913) Elizabethan Rogues and Vagabonds. Oxford: Claredon.

CRAPSEY, E. (1872) The Nether Side of New York. New York: Sheldon.

INCIARDI, J. A. (1977) "In search of the class cannon: A field study of professional pickpockets," in R. S. Weppner (ed.) Street Ethnography. Beverly Hills, CA: Sage.

———(1975) Careers in Crime. Chicago: Rand McNally.

JUDGES, A. V. (1930) The Elizabethan Underworld. London: Routledge.

MARTIN, E. W. (1868) Secrets of the Great City. Philadelphia: National.

MAURER, D. W. (1964) Whiz Mob. New Haven: College and University Press.

VILES, E. and F. J. FURNIVALL [eds.] (1880) The Rogues and Vagabonds of Shakespeare's Youth. London: N. Truber.

SUTHERLAND, E. H. (1937) The Professional Thief. Chicago: University of Chicago Press.

WHEATLEY, H. B. and P. CUNNINGHAM (1891) London Life, Past and Present, Vol. 3. London: John Murray.

Jay S. Albanese

Niagara University

3

GOD AND THE MAFIA REVISITED
From Valachi to Fratianno

Like the existence of God, the nature of organized crime in North America has been based largely on unprovable assertions. It was 1969 when Gordon Hawkins originally put forth this argument, which has gained increasing acceptance over the last 15 years. The substance of the analogy lies in the similarity of arguments used to explain both God and the Mafia.

> Yet if the evidence of an ALL-AMERICAN crime confederation or syndicate is both suspect and tenuous to the point of nullity, it is clear that for the believer there is nothing that could count decisively against the assertion that it exists. Thus, denials of membership in, or knowledge of, the syndicate can not only be dismissed as self-evidently false, but also adduced as evidence of what they deny. If there is gang warfare, this indicates that "an internal struggle for dominance over the entire organization" is going on; and also provides "a somber illustration of how cruel and calculating the underworld continues to be." If peace prevails this may be taken either as evidence of the power of the syndicate leadership and the fear in which it is held; or alternatively as reflecting the development of "the sophisticated and polished control of rackets that now characterize that organization."

Hawkins concludes,

> In the end, it is difficult to resist the conclusion that one is not dealing with an empirical phenomenon at all, but with an article of faith, transcending the contingent particularity of everyday experience and logically unassailable; one of those reassuring popular demonologies that, William Buckley has remarked, the successful politician has to cherish and preserve and may, in the end, come to believe [1969: 50-51].

43

Neither Hawkins nor I maintains that organized crime does not exist. To believe this would mean that all crime is the product of the random or unplanned acts of individuals. Clearly, this is not the case. The point Hawkins attempted to make was that although belief in God relies essentially on faith, believers in a North American "Mafia" or 'La Cosa Nostra" expect others also to believe it based on a similar leap of faith.

At the time of Hawkins's writing in 1969, the only "independent" evidence that had been produced in support of a North American criminal conspiracy was the testimony of Joseph Valachi in 1963. Valachi was a criminal who became a government informant and testified to the existence of a nationwide criminal conspiracy which he said controlled the bulk of the illegal gambling, prostitution, and narcotics trade in North America. Although the 1967 President's Crime Commission, and many subsequent writers, have accepted Valachi's description of organized crime as fact, Hawkins and others including Dwight Smith (1975), Alan Block (1978), and Humbert Nelli (1981), have pointed to a number of inconsistencies that cast doubt on the veracity of Valachi's testimony. For example, if Valachi's story was true, why had no one ever heard of La Cosa Nostra before he testified? Why did his "revelations" prove to be of little value in criminal prosecutions? Why have subsequent historical inquiries been unable to corroborate Valachi's account of a national "Castellammarese War" which was said to have resulted in the establishment of La Cosa Nostra? Why were law enforcement officials unable to construct their charts of organized crime "families" independent of Valachi? These, and other, unaccountable aspects of Valachi's testimony make him a rather weak foundation on which to base a belief in a North American criminal conspiracy. As Hawkins recognized,

> [Valachi's testimony] was neither consistent with itself nor with other evidence presented to the Committee. Valachi both contradicted himself and was contradicted by others. Moreover, what the Attorney General called "the biggest intelligence breakthrough yet" appears to have produced nothing in the way of tangible results [1969: 46].

NEW EVIDENCE?

In 1980, this debate over the true nature of organized crime was rekindled with the introduction of another criminal-turned-government-informant, Jimmy Fratianno. The testimony of Fratianno was seen by many as being more important than Valachi's because, unlike Valachi, Fratianno was said to be (1) a high-ranking member of an organized criminal group, and (2) his testimony appeared to be resulting in the conviction of a number of suspected organized criminals.

As a result, it is now appropriate to update Hawkins's original thesis to determine whether or not the uncorroborated assertions of Valachi have been supported or refuted by Fratianno. Even more important, evidence used in support of Fratianno's testimony will be examined. It is hoped that analyses such as this will begin to provide some closure to discussions of the true nature of organized crime and will allow future investigations to place greater emphasis on issues such as its etiology and the evaluation of public policy measures designed to combat it.

THE TIERI TRIAL

Although Fratianno has testified at several trials that have ended in convictions, only one has been selected for discussion here. The case of U.S. v. Frank Tieri took place in federal court in Manhattan in 1980. After a month-long trial, Frank Tieri was convicted of racketeering and conspiracy and was, according to court records, the first person ever proven to be 'boss" of a Cosa Nostra "family." This case was selected for examination here, not only for the significance of the conviction, but also for its focus on proving the existence of a national conspiracy of organized criminals.

Frank Tieri was originally indicted on charges of racketeering, conspiracy, bankruptcy fraud, and income tax evasion. He was charged under the Racketeer Influenced and Corrupt Organization (RICO) provisions of the Organized Crime Control Act of 1970. Under this statute, it is illegal to acquire, operate, or receive income from an "enterprise" through a "pattern" of "racketeering activity." Therefore, any individual or group who commits two or more indictable offenses characteristic of organized crime within a 10-year period (the "pattern"), as part of a continuing criminal enterprise, can receive extended penalties of up to 20 years imprisonment, fines up to $25,000, forfeiture of any interest in the enterprise, as well as civil damages and dissolution of the enterprise itself. The courts have since interpreted "racketeering activity" to encompass *any* indictable offense punishable by a year or more imprisonment.

The reason why this statute is particularly important to the Tieri case is that the "enterprise" he was alleged to have illegally operated or received income from was La Cosa Nostra. According to the indictment, the grand jury alleged that

> a criminal organization known by various names including La Cosa Nostra was a criminal group which operated throughout the United States through entities known as "Families" with each such "Family" having as its leader a person known as a "Boss."

> At all times relevant to this Indictment, the defendant Frank Tieri, a.k.a. "Funzi Tiera," a.k.a. "Funzuola," a.k.a. "The Old Man," was the "boss" of one of the five New York City "Families" of La Cosa Nostra and which "Family" constituted and continues to constitute an "enterprise," as defined by [the Organized Crime Control Act of 1970].

The significance of this case, therefore, lies in its attempt to prove the existence of La Cosa Nostra as a continuing illegal enterprise, that Tieri was the boss of one of its families, and that he committed various organized crimes in that capacity.

Fratianno's role in the case was not merely to testify to the existence of La Cosa Nostra, but also to implicate Tieri in at least two indictable offenses during the last 10 years in order to establish the pattern of racketeering activity necessary for a conviction under RICO. One of the illegal acts Fratianno testified to was Tieri's alleged involvement in a bankruptcy fraud of the Westchester Premier Theater in New York State. The presiding federal trial judge acknowledged during a conversation with prosecution and defense counsel (while the jury was excused) how important Fratianno's testimony was to the prosecution's case, and how much the jury had to rely on his fragmentary testimony.

> COURT: This is a hard subject which keeps coming up, and it's very hard for me to assess this thing. It may be that Mr. Goldberg (defense counsel) is way overdoing this, in his espousal of this theory (that certain key FBI photographs were missing), but right at the moment I don't think he is, and I don't think it is overdoing it. I think that—I assume that the Westchester thing is an essential part of the government's case . . . . The Westchester County theater case, you have to prove it in order to succeed on counts 1 and 2, don't you?

> MR. ACKERMAN (Prosecutor): Sure, I agree.

> COURT: It's one of several but it's an essential, and the connection with Tieri with it is essential, so it is very, very important, and it's a win or lose proposition. We keep having this thing surface.

So, this may be absolutely far out, but I wonder if there is some-body who really is an expert on the relationship crime families who could—you see, I don't really know. I know nothing about the sub-ject virtually, and I don't know whether it is part of the protocol or part of the custom and usage to have two families involved in one operation. Now, there was that very fragmentary testimony of Fra-tianno. You know, it's two questions or one question or whatever, and it doesn't solve very much. He said what he said. But it's almost a subject you'd like a Yale professor to come in and . . .

MR. GOLDERG: Harvard.

COURT: Harvard. You know, I will take any one of those modern schools, and come in and explain to me—I would like to know.

MR. GOLDBERG: Maybe I can do it. I was on both sides.

COURT: But what is it, because it may be that people who know about this know that it is impossible to have a situation where you've got the kind of relationship the government is talking about. Maybe that's just an impossibility. On the other hand, maybe there is enough of a fraternity between the different families, if they are families, there is enough of a fraternity that they go to each other's wakes, they will go to each other's theatres, they will lend each other money, and if Frank Sinatra comes to the Westchester Premier Theatre it wouldn't be unusual to have Mr. Tieri, who is not a high profile type, he is in the background controlling it, maybe the Gambino people are a little more, you know, social, and they go to the theatre and they get photographed with Sinatra and all this goes on. Maybe this is perfectly standard. I haven't the faintest idea, and what do I have? That's a one-liner.

It's a one-liner by Mr. Fratianno. I don't know [U.S. v Tieri, 1980: 2181-2183].

Later that same day, the trial was nearing completion, but the pro-secutor's request to charge (i.e., recommendations to the judge for his legal instructions to the jury for their deliberations) claimed that Fratianno's testimony about the Westchester case was *not* essential for conviction.

COURT: Incidentally, you know, one thing we talked about this morn-ing, and I hadn't really started to work on the charge, and I wasn't going to, but I asked if the Westchester Premier Theatre matter was an essential. But according to your request to charge—

MR. ACKERMAN: No, it is not essential.

COURT: —You said yes to me this morning.

MR. ACKERMAN: It is only on one count, it is essential, obviously, and one predicate act. It is only one of the acts of racketeering of six that are charged.

COURT: And your contention is you only have to—

MR. ACKERMAN: Prove two.

COURT: —Prove two; is that right?

MR. ACKERMAN: Yes.

MR. GOLDBERG: Judge, before he offers an expert, will he have an offer of proof?

COURT: You mean expert testimony by Cantalupo?

MR. GOLDBERG: No. He's going to have expert testimony by an FBI agent about the interrelationship of families, no doubt plugging up the holes created by Mr. Fratianno.

COURT: He didn't say that.

MR. ACKERMAN: No.

COURT: No [U.S. v. Tieri, 1980: 2304-2305].

It can be seen from these two excerpts from the trial record that there were shifting views regarding the importance of Fratianno's testimony before and then after he testified. (It also should be noted that prior to trial, defense counsel Jay Goldberg sought to have the prosecutor disqualified from this case. A letter Ackerman submitted to the U.S. Parole Commission asking for Fratianno's early release from prison claimed that Fratianno's testimony led to the conviction of four persons in an earlier case involving fraud at the Westchester Premier Theatre. Goldberg pointed out that no one was convicted at the trial in which Fratianno testified. The presiding judge, Thomas Greisa, defied this motion to disqualify the prosecutor, however.) It is clear from these incidents that the credibility of Fratianno's testimony had not been well established at this point.

DOES LA COSA NOSTRA EXIST?

Perhaps the most important aspect of the Tieri case was the government's effort to prove the existence of La Cosa Nostra. This effort was based entirely on the testimony of Fratianno.

MR. ACKERMAN: Now, directing your attention to late 1947, early 1946, did you become a member of any organization?

MR. FRATIANNO: Yes, sir.

MR. ACKERMAN: What is the name of that organization?

MR. FRATIANNO: La Cosa Nostra.

MR. ACKERMAN: How long have you been a member of La Cosa Nostra?

MR. FRATIANNO: Thirty-two years, sir.

MR. ACKERMAN: Would you tell the jury what La Cosa Nostra is?

MR. FRATIANNO: Well, I would say it is a secret organization, sir.

MR. ACKERMAN: What does it do, primarily?

MR. FRATIANNO: Well, it engages in different businesses, illegal activities.

MR. ACKERMAN: What kinds of illegal activities?

MR. FRATIANNO: I'd say shylocking, bookmaking, taking bets on horses, football games, baseball games, labor racketeering, all sorts of illegal activity...

MR. ACKERMAN: Mr. Fratianno, would you please tell the jury what requirements there are for one to become a member of La Cosa Nostra?

MR. FRATIANNO: Well, you are more or less proposed by somebody. Sometimes you do something significant. Then there is times when you have a brother or father in it, and you get in that way. There's different ways, sir.

MR. ACKERMAN: Is there any kind of background requirement that's necessary?

MR. FRATIANNO: You have to be Italian, sir.

MR. ACKERMAN: Would you please tell the jury where La Cosa Nostra is located?

MR. FRATIANNO: Well, it is located in different parts of the United States, sir, most of the big cities.

MR. ACKERMAN: How is this national organization broken down with respect to the big cities?

MR. FRATIANNO: It is broken down into families, sir.

MR. ACKERMAN: Now, I am am going to put a map of the United States which has been marked as Government's Exhibit 4 for identification. Mr. Fratianno, starting from the West Coast, could you tell the jury where there are families, and which cities have families of La Cosa Nostra? [U.S. v. Tieri, 1980:863, 870].

Fratianno went on to claim that "families" of La Cosa Nostra exist in San Francisco, San Jose, Los Angeles, Denver, Dallas, Kansas City (Missouri), Chicago, Detroit, Cleveland, Buffalo, St. Louis, Pittsburgh, Steubenville (Ohio), Milwaukee, Philadelphia, Pittson (Pennsylvania), New Orleans, Tampa, a city in Connecticut, Providence, and five families in New York City. He also testified that he met Frank Tieri in 1976, when Tieri was boss of one of the New York City families.

Unfortunately, problems with Fratianno's account of La Cosa Nostra begin here. The head of the FBI's organized crime operations testified before the Senate Permanent Subcommittee on Investigations in April, 1980 and said there exist 26 "active" families of La Cosa Nostra (LCN) in the United States. Interestingly, he claimed there were LCN families in Tucson (Arizona), Rockford (Illinois), Madison (Wisconsin), and Elizabeth-Newark (New Jersey) that Fratianno did not acknowledge. Further, he did not acknowledge that any families existed in Steubenville or in Connecticut, or that there was an active group in Dallas as Fratianno had testified (U.S. Senate, 1980: 114-116).

A comparison of the Fratianno and FBI testimony in 1980, compared with Valachi's 1963 testimony about the cities where LCN 'families" supposedly exist, reveals some further unaccountable differences.

MR. ALDERMAN (Counsel to the Senate Committee): Mr. Valachi, we have covered New York rather extensively. Now are there any other members, any other families outside of the area of New York?

MR. VALACHI: You mean like Chicago, Boston?

MR. ALDERMAN: Yes. Could you mention the cities where other families exist of the Cosa Nostra, and if you know, the numbers of the members as you know them, could you mention them?

MR. VALACHI: I will start with Philadelphia. In Philadelphia I would say about a hundred. Boston, when I left the streets, was about 20, 18 or 20. Chicago, about 150. Cleveland, about 40 or 50. Los Angeles, about 40. Tampa, about 10. Newark, about a hundred. Detroit, I am not familiar at all with Detroit . . .

MR. ALDERMAN: How about Buffalo?

MR. VALACHI: Buffalo, about 100 to 125.

MR. ALDERMAN: Utica, N.Y.?

MR. VALACHI: Utica, 80 to 100.

MR. ALDERMAN: I think you covered New Orleans, did you?

MR. VALACHI: No, I didn't cover New Orleans. Very few in New Orleans.

MR. ALDERMAN: Now you mentioned you don't know any in Detroit. Do you know if any families exist there?

MR. VALACHI: Yes, they exist.

MR. ALDERMAN: But do you know the number they have there?

MR. VALACHI: I have no idea of Detroit.

MR. ADLERMAN: Did you mention Tampa?

MR. VALACHI: Tampa, I did, yes, about 10. When I left the streets.

MR. ALDERMAN: In other words, the 10 cities (sic) are Boston, Chicago, Los Angeles, San Francisco, New Orleans, Tampa, Buffalo, Utica, Philadelphia, Cleveland, and Detroit?

MR. VALACHI: Right [U.S. Senate, 1963: 386-387].

Counting the five New York City families, Valachi identified a total of 16 LCN groups in the United States. Fratianno dropped two cities from Valachi's list but added nine others, for a total of 25 LCN cities. Further, the FBI testified to the existence of 26 LCN groups, disagreeing with two of the cities Fratianno included, while adding four others. The disparate claims of Valachi, Fratianno, and the FBI are summarized in Table 3.1.

Whether one chooses to believe Fratianno or the FBI, the number of LCN groups has apparently increased from between 40% to 60% since 1963. If this is true, however, their subsequent testimony as to the size of La Cosa Nostra must be false.

At the beginning of the same 1980 Senate hearings, the FBI director and his unit chief responsible for organized crime investigations gave testimony as to the family structure and size of La Cosa Nostra.

SENATOR COHEN: May I also ask for a clarification for the record that, when you say "families" that does not necessarily intimate they are blood relations, although there may be blood relations within the "family"—

MR. NELSON: (FBI unit chief): That is correct, there may be blood

TABLE 3.1   Cities Where Families of La Cosa Nostra
Are Alleged to Exist

Valachi (1963)	Fratianno (1980)	FBI (1980)
Boston	xx	Boston-Providence
Buffalo	Buffalo	Buffalo
Chicago	Chicago	Chicago
Cleveland	Cleveland	Cleveland
Detroit	Detroit	Detroit
Los Angeles	Los Angeles	Los Angeles
New York	New York	New York
(5 families)	(5 families)	(5 families)
New Orleans	New Orleans	New Orleans
Philadelphia	Philadelphia	Philadelphia
San Francisco	San Francisco	San Francisco
Tampa	Tampa	Tampa
Utica, NY	xx	xx
xx	San Jose	San Jose
xx	Denver	Denver-Pueblo
xx	Dallas	(Inactive)
xx	Kansas City, MO	Kansas City, MO
xx	Pittsburgh	Pittsburgh
xx	Steubenville, OH	xx
xx	Milwaukee	Milwaukee
xx	Connecticut (1 city)	xx
xx	Providence, RI	(See Boston)
xx	St. Louis	St. Louis
xx	Pittston, PA	Pittston-Cranston- Wilkes-Barre, PA
xx	xx	Tucson
xx	xx	Springfield, IL (inactive)
xx	xx	Rockford, IL
xx	xx	Madison, WI
xx	xx	Elizabeth-Newark, NJ

xx = no family reported.

relationships, but "family" comes from the Italian "famiglia"and
it does not necessarily mean that they are blood related. In most cases,
of course, they are not.

MR. STEINBERG (Counsel to the Senate Committee): Mr. Nelson, how
many members of La Cosa Nostra exist today?

MR. NELSON: There are approximately 2,000 members. However, I
must say that is probably the most misleading figure I could throw
out because these are the initiated members, the people who are con-

sidered by other people as part of the organization.

Our most conservative estimate is that for every initiated member, there are approximately at least 10 people aligned with them and associated with them on a daily basis whose day-to-day activities are criminal and associated with La Cosa Nostra.

So the conservative figure of the number of people in this country who are doing La Cosa Nostra's work is 20,000, and that is conservative [U.S. Senate, 1980: 90-91, 19].

Compare this 1980 description of the size of La Cosa Nostra with Valachi's original descripton in 1963.

MR. ALDERMAN: Mr. Valachi, along those lines, how many active members do you feel there are in the New York area that belong to the various families? . . . All of the five families.

MR. VALACHI: About 2,000.

MR. ALDERMAN: Those whom you have been able to identify in the five families, you have marked with stars on these charts?

MR. VALACHI: Yes.

MR. ALDERMAN: But they do not represent all of the members of the families? I mean in any family you don't know all of the members of the family?

MR. VALACHI: Well, I tell you, I am off of the streets for about 4 years. I am sure I know more than what I have got up there.

MR. ALDERMAN: These charts portray something over 400 names.

MR. VALACHI: Something like that.

MR. ALDERMAN: You say there are 2,000 members. So there are quite a number of members whom you do not know.

MR. VALACHI: Yes, there is quite a number, yes.

MR. ALDERMAN: How many inactive members are there?

MR. VALACHI: I would say about 2,500 or 3,000.

MR. ALDERMAN: You are just talking about New York City alone?

MR. VALACHI: I am talking about New York, including Newark [U.S. Senate, 1963: 270-271].

If Valachi estimates LCN membership in the New York City area alone to be 2,000 in 1963, and the FBI says that the *nationwide* membership is only 2,000 in 1980, how can we consider organized crime to be an increasing threat? Even if we choose to accept both Valachi's and the FBI's *upper* estimates of LCN participants, a New York City-only membership of 5,000 in 1963, compared to a nationwide estimate of 20,000 in 1980, certainly does not indicate growth in the size of La Cosa Nostra (considering that the FBI counts only five New York City families out of a nationwide total of 26).

It is difficult to understand, therefore, the Justice Department's request at the 1980 hearings for additional investigative tools to make it easier to prosecute alleged organized criminals. At these hearings, the Senate was asked to allow sentence reductions for convicted felons who offer to testify for the government *at any time* during the course of their incarceration. The Senate was also asked to revise the Tax Reform Act of 1976 and the Right to Financial Privacy Act to make it easier to obtain an individual's tax and bank records for investigative purposes. These and other legislative requests appear out of line with the Justice Department's own testimony about the size of La Cosa Nostra. As the FBI claimed in 1980,

> Without a doubt, in our estimation, the group known as La Cosa Nostra is the most powerful organized crime group in this country. It is first in an organized criminal ranking, that has no second or third. No one else is close [U.S. Senate, 1980: 87].

This is difficult to understand when the Justice Department's earlier witness, Joseph Valachi, said in 1963 that the size of La Cosa Nostra was certainly no larger than it was reported to be in 1980. Furthermore, if the LCN has not increased in size between 1963 and 1980, how could it have established families in 7 to 10 additional cities during that period? As a result, there not only appear to be contradictions between Fratianno and the FBI's testimony in 1980, but the Justice Department claims about La Cosa Nostra in 1980 cannot be believed if we are also expected to believe the claims of their 1963 witness, Joseph Valachi.

A final note of concern relates to how La Cosa Nostra is supposedly organized. At the Tieri trial, Fratianno testified about the organization of LCN families.

> MR. ACKERMAN: Now, is there any structure in La Cosa Nostra above the families which are located in the cities as we have in Government's Exhibit 4?
>
> MR. FRATIANNO: Yes, sir.

MR. ACKERMAN: What is the name of that structure?

MR. FRATIANNO: Well, they have a commission, sir.

MR. ACKERMAN: Now, who comprises the commission?

MR. FRATIANNO: The five bosses of the New York family plus the boss of the Chicago family, sir.

MR. ACKERMAN: Now, what is the purpose of the commission?

MR. FRATIANNO: Well, they more or less handle disputes with other families. If you have a problem with another family, they more or less handle it, sir.

MR. ACKERMAN: Now, when a new boss is selected by a family, who is notified?

MR. FRATIANNO: The commission is notified, sir.

MR. ACKERMAN: Would you describe to the jury how a family of La Cosa Nostra is actually run?

MR. FRATIANNO: Well, it's run by the boss. He's the main one. And then they have an underboss. They have a consigliere, and then they have capos . . .

MR. ACKERMAN: What is the consigliere's job in the family?

MR. FRATIANNO: Well, he is more or less the counselor of the family, you know.

MR. ACKERMAN: You mentioned the capos. What are they?

MR. FRATIANNO: Well, they are like captains. They more or less— they break the soldiers into units and they belong to the capos, certain capos.

MR. ACKERMAN: You referred to soldiers. Is everybody who is not a capo, a boss, underboss, and consigliere, a soldier in La Cosa Nostra?

MR. FRATIANNO: That's correct [U.S. v. Tieri, 1980: 875-878].

Therefore, each family has ranks from "'soldier" up to "boss," and the families are, according to Fratianno, regulated by a six-member commission of six family bosses (of the five New York City families and Chicago). When the FBI unit chief testified before the Senate in 1980, however, he arrived at a different formulation.

At that time [when the commission was allegedly formed in 1931], there were seven members on the Mafia Commission, the La Cosa Nostra Commission . . . Currently, there are nine. It is made up of the five bosses of the New York families, the boss in Philadelphia, the boss in Buffalo, the boss in Detroit, and the boss in Chicago [U.S. Senate, 1980: 88].

This confusion over the existence and size of the "commission" is further amplified when Fratinno's 1981 biography offers still a *third* version of the commission structure. In it, the commission is said to be composed of 10 Cosa Nostra bosses. Fratianno's credibility suffers again, not only due to his self-contradiction but also because he admits in his biography that he was told of the family and commission structure by someone else in 1947 (Demaris, 1981: 20-22). This inconsistency is especially disturbing because Fratianno claims he was the one-time boss of the Los Angeles family. Therefore, Fratianno's testimony on this subject is not only inconsistent, but it is also hearsay.

WHAT DOES IT ALL MEAN?

This chapter has addressed only the basic structure of Fratianno's testimony about La Cosa Nostra. It is clear from this sampling, however, that his testimony sheds little light on an accurate understanding of organized crime. At other points during the Tieri trial, Fratianno was found to have contradicted his prior grand jury testimony, admitted violation of the family code in setting up a fellow member to be murdered, admitted lying under oath in the past, and admitted defrauding the FBI while receiving money as a paid informant. These facts, in addition to his unsavory background, do not serve to enhance his credibility.

Nevertheless, Frank Tieri was ultimately convicted of racketeering and conspiracy, undoubtedly due to the testimony of other witnesses at the trial and the failure of the defense to call a single witness in Tieri's behalf. Only through interviews with the other participants in the case, including the judge, prosecutor, defense counsel, and jury, will a more satisfactory explanation for Tieri's conviction emerge. This is not likely to happen, however, because Tieri died only three months after his conviction in March 1981 at age 77. Tieri's poor health was cited throughout the trial by his counsel as preventing him from coherently conversing with Tieri and therefore interfered with the preparation of an adequate defense.

A conviction cannot stand, of course, when death has deprived an offender the opportunity to appeal his conviction. As a result, Tieri's indictment was formally dismissed and the conviction vacated in May 1981.

THE POWER OF UNFOUNDED
BUT POPULAR BELIEFS

The lack of any reliable evidence in support of a belief in a nation-wide criminal organization called La Cosa Nostra or Mafia makes it difficult to understand the continued belief in one by many law enforcement officials and the general public. In fact, the available objective evidence has continually eroded the basis for any belief in such a criminal organization. Putting aside Fratianno's contradictions, investigations of the possibility that a Mafia or Cosa Nostra emigrated from Italy or Sicily to North America have uncovered no evidence that a criminal organization of this type exists, or ever existed, in Italy (Albini, 1971; Block, 1974; Hess, 1973; Servadio, 1978). Further, those that claim a Mafia or Cosa Nostra emerged from a 1930s gangland war in the United States have found no support among objective investigators of this claim (Block, 1980; Nelli, 1981; Smith, 1975). As Albini has noted, even a recent Italian parliamentary commission in Sicily has concluded that no secret society called the Mafia exists there. The testimony of an expert witness for this Italian commission investigation brings us back to Hawkins's original argument.

> The Mafia as we say is comparable to God; it's something that exists, therefore it exists, we know that, but where is God? In all places; God is in the air, in front of us, God is in all objects. But where is the Mafia? Where is God? We believe by faith [cited in Albini, 1978: 289].

Unfortunately, the testimony of Jimmy Fratianno brings us no closer to a true understanding of organized crime in North America than did Valachi 20 years earlier. Although the power of ideological beliefs can be very strong in preventing the reception of new evidence inconsistent with prevailing views (Albanese, 1982; Albini, 1978), it is time perhaps that we heeded the call for the objective and systematic study of the social and economic realities of organized crime (Ianni and Reuss-Ianni, 1980; Sacco, 1980; Smith, 1982). Only in this way will our public policy decisions be based on accurately defined problems, rather than a witch hunt for an elusive organization that may have been invented only to mask our desire for the illicit goods and services it supposedly provides—or to provide the government with a scapegoat to divert public attention away from further shrinkage of the right to privacy and the social and economic problems that truly cause organized crime. As Hawkins suggests, the intensive study of organized crime is long overdue and should begin "preferably without too many preconceptions."

REFERENCES

ALBANESE, J. S. (1982) Organizational Offenders: Why Solutions Fail to Political, Corporate, and Organized Crime. Niagara Falls, NY: Apocalypse Publishing.

ALBINI J. L. (1971) The American Mafia: Genesis of a Legend. New York: Appleton Century-Crofts.

———and B. J. Bajon (1978) "Witches, mafia, mental illness and social reality: a study in the power of mythical belief." International Journal of Criminology and Penology 6: 285-294.

BLOCK, A. A. (1980) East Side—West Side: Organizing Crime in New York, 1930-1950. Cardiff, Wales: University College Cardiff Press.

———(1978) "History and the Study of Organized Crime." Urban Life 6: 455-474.

BLOK, A. (1974) The Mafia of a Sicilian Village, 1860-1960. New York: Harper & Row.

DEMARIS, O. (1981) The Last Mafioso. New York: Bantam.

HAWKINS, G. (1969) "God and the Mafia." The Public Interest 14: 24-51.

HESS, H. (1973) Mafia and Mafiosi: The Structure of Power. Lexington, MA: D.C. Heath.

IANNI, F. A. J. and E. REUSS-IANNI (1980) "Organized crime: a social and economic perspective," pp. 294-312 in G. R. Newman (ed.) Crime and Deviance: A Comparative Perspective. Beverly Hills, CA: Sage.

NELLI, H. S. (1981) The Business of Crime: Italians and Syndicate Crime in the United States. Chicago: University of Chicago Press.

SACCO, V. F. (1980) "An approach to the study of organized crime" pp. 248-264 in R.A. Silverman and J.J. Teevan, Jr. (eds.) Crime in Canadian Society. Toronto: Butterworth & Co.

SERVADIO, G. (1978) Mafioso: A History of the Mafia from its Origins to the Present Day. New York: Dell.

SMITH, D. C. (1982) "White-collar crime, organized crime, and the business establishment: resolving a crisis in criminological theory," pp. 23-38 in P. Wickman and T. Dailey, (eds.) White-Collar and Economic Crime. Lexington, MA: D.C. Heath.

———(1975) The Mafia Mystique. New York: Basic Books.

U.S. Senate Committee on Governmental Affairs (1980) Permanent Subcommittee on Investigations. Organized Crime and Use of Violence—Hearings Part 1. 96th Congress, Second Session. Washington, DC: Government Printing Office.

———(1963)Permanent Subcommittee on Investigations. Organized Crime and Illicit Traffic in Narcotics—Hearings Part 1. 88th Congress, 1st Session. Washington, DC: Government Printing Office.

U.S. v. FRANK TIERI (1980) Trial Transcript. United States District Court Southern District of New York 80 Cr. 381.

Peter A. Lupsha
University of New Mexico

4

NETWORKS VERSUS NETWORKING
Analysis of an Organized Crime Group

When Daniel Bell wrote his now classic article, "Crime as an American Way of Life" (1953) and expounded the "queer ladder thesis" that organized crime was simply another form of upward mobility and that ethnic succession would soon replace one ethnic crime organization with another, he could not have known this viewpoint would soon become academic orthodoxy. The fact that the queer ladder thesis and the ethnic succession model were so readily accepted by upwardly mobile academics and ethnics is not as suprising as the fact that few of these intellectuals sought to question its empirical accuracy.

Organized crime is a difficult phenomenon to study, and many academics view all vested authority—particularly law enforcement—with skepticism. So perhaps it is understandable that only limited empirical research on organized crime was undertaken in the decades following popularization of the Bell article in his *The End of Ideology* and its regular reprinting in sociology and criminology textbooks. What research that did occur tended to substantiate and reinforce the Bell perspectives. Dwight Smith, Jr. (1975) wrote that organized crime was a part of the ethnic bias of law enforcement and rested in "an alien conspiracy" mentality. The works of Donald Cressey (1969) and Ralph Salerno (Salerno and Tompkins, 1969) were criticized or often ignored for being overly bureaucratic and structural, and too close to the government task force reports. Scholars like Joseph Albini (1971) attempted to find a middle ground with a theory of "patron-client" relationships, as did historians like Mark Haller (1971) and Humbert S. Nelli (1976). Others, such as Francis A.J. Ianni (1972, 1974, 1978) and, later, Annelise Anderson (1979), corroborated the Bell model of ethnic succession, the emergence of a "Black Mafia," and provided a general view that organized crime was increasingly respectable, less threatening or violent. They and others, like Peter Reuter and Jonathan Rubinstein (1978; Reuter et al., 1981), both stressed the inefficiencies and ineptitude of organized criminals, along with popular myths and the over-dramatic coverage given to organized crime by law enforcement, the press, and journalists in articles and books. William J. Chambliss (1978) and Alan Block (Chambliss and Block, 1981), after conducting both observational and detailed historical research, recently joined forces to show that not only were La Cosa Nostra, Italian-American crime perspectives overdrawn, but that organized crime was more a product of the contradictions of capitalism and the American economy than other forces. In this, Marxist sociologists and criminologists heartily agreed (Quinney, 1978). The work of economist Thomas Schelling and others—for example, the readings of Lawrence Kaplan and Dennis Kessler (1976), and more recently the work of Simon and Witte (1982) and Luksetich and White (1982)—all furthered the view that organized crime can be better understood as a function of markets, demand factors, value conflicts, and overregulation in our society.

All of these scholars applying their different models, perspectives, data bases, and analyses have added substantially to our knowledge of the phenomenon of organized crime. It is impossible to say they all are right, but in one aspect or another they are. And it is from this mix that we have gained our increased understanding of organized crime. Using the many ideas their work provides, I will attempt now to define organized crime and its key conceptual elements.

A DEFINITION OF ORGANIZED CRIME

Organized crime is an activity, by a group of individuals, who consciously develop task roles and specializations, patterns of interaction, statuses, and relationships, spheres of accountability and responsibility; and who with continuity over time engage in acts legal and illegal usually involving (a) large amounts of capital, (b) buffers (nonmember associates), (c) the use of violence or the threat of violence (actual or perceived), (d) the corruption of public officials, their agents, or those in positions of responsibility and trust. This activity is goal oriented and develops sequentially over time. Its purpose is the accumulaton of large sums of capital and influence, along with minimization of risk.

Capital acquired (black untaxed monies) are in part processed (laundered) into legitimate sectors of the economy through the use of multiple fronts and buffers to the end of increased influence, power, capital and enhanced potential for criminal gain with increasingly minimized risk.

While not all of the scholars cited would agree with this definition, they would all agree on the need for empirical research. This definition can assist the development of such research for it can be broken into a number of conceptual elements each of which can, along with derivative propositions and hypotheses, be used empirically to study and examine occurrences of organized crime and its enterprises.

Key Definitional Elements Facilitating Empirical Analysis

(1) An activity.

(2) An over-time developmental activity (sequential).

(3) Possessing roles, functions, statuses, and relationships.

(4) Possessing role hierarchies; specializations and division of labor

(5) Careerist (life-time) activity and often group membership.

(6) Nonmember associates and buffers.

(7) Corruption of public and private authority, its agents, persons in positions of trust.

(8) Use of violence or threat of violence (real or perceived).

(9) Criminal processes, activity or enterprises.

(10) Capital activities (i.e., paper trails).

(11) Influence activities (i.e., corruption, pressure trails).

(12) Individual structural components, and constraints patterning individual crime matrices. This permits both individual enterprise and comparative analysis of that enterprise.

(13) A number of different crime matrices, each with their individual signature, for either enterprise or comparative study.

(14) A number of different organized crime groups with varying backgrounds and openness or rigidity of structure.

(15) An inherent logic, rationality, and instrumentality to the acts, activity, and purpose of the group.

These definitional elements not only make possible empirical analysis of organized crime groups, they can be used to develop further concepts for proposition construction and hypothesis testing.

ACADEMIC VERSUS LAW ENFORCEMENT (LE):
ANALYTICAL PERSPECTIVES

The differences between the academician studying organized crime and the law enforcement intelligence analysts are not as large as one might initially think. The most important single difference is that while the academic tends to take a theoretical issue and use empirical analysis to pinpoint that problem for the organized crime group as a whole, the law enforcement intelligence analyst often has his focus chosen for him and is directed in the analysis of the target by the goal of prosecution (making a case against the crime group). The case-target-prosecution approach requires that the LE analyst cannot follow interesting research directions that may not be germane to the current investigation, while the academic retains that luxury. The second difference is that the academic also possesses the luxury of time. The LE analyst must often produce an intelligence product in an extremely limited time frame, while the academic generally operates with more leisurely deadlines.

In the organized crime area, the law enforcement analyst often possesses certain real advantages that the academic lacks, and these should be noted. First, the data base the LE intelligence analyst has to work with is theoretically more complete and more current than that which the academic normally has access to. Second, the intelligence analyst can get field investigative corroboration and new data from staff investigators and the larger law enforcement intelligence network. The academic studying organized crime does not have that access or data follow-up control, and so must work with weaker data sets, qualifying assumptions, and information gaps that the law enforcement intelligence analyst does not necessarily have to face.

These are real differences, and they have real consequences. They do not mean, however, that the long-range objectives of these research efforts are different. Indeed, it can be argued that certain intelligence analysis units—particularly at the federal level—should devote some resources to going beyond the case-target-prosecution approach.[1] For in organized crime cases such an approach may only put away individuals and open positions for more aggressive, upwardly mobile younger members of the crime group. The success of the case-target-prosecution approach may remove stable leadership figures, creating situations of lethal competition and conflict as well as undermining established law enforcement "snitch" and informant systems.

Unfortunately, many law enforcement units have neither the time nor the expertise to carry out such essentially strategic intelligence studies of organized crime. This cost of a tactical, operational-only approach in law enforcement can be a telling one for both the agency and the public. For without good foreknowledge, which is what intelligence is all about, law enforcement can be trapped in a reactive posture of post facto collection, prosecution-oriented analysis, and dragnet "vacuum cleaner" approaches to collection that can injure innocent citizens by abusing their civil rights and liberties. As this chapter will show, the higher quality intelligence analysis, more cost-efficient use of collection resources, oversight, and evaluation of informant systems, more accurate and effective targeting of suspects, and in-court prosecution of organized crime groups can occur through the use of strategic intelligence analytical approaches. The particular approach used here is network analysis, but other formats of strategic intelligence and analysis such as threat analysis, aggressiveness analysis, and vulnerability analysis should also be incorporated into the daily methodologies of law enforcement dealing with organized crime (Lupsha, 1980).

NETWORKS VERSUS NETWORKING

Many law enforcement intelligence analysts have received some training in "link analysis." This is the process of constructing networks in which the Anacapa Sciences Inc. corporation trains thousands of law enforcement officers each year. The purpose of such programs is to bring logic and scientific method to criminal investigations. Typically, the types of analysis taught in this network approach consists of the following:

—*Link analysis*: to show the ties, in a schematic format, among individuals and organizations.

—*Event analysis*: which develops the over-time series of relationships among actors and criminal acts.

—*Flow analysis*: to illustrate the movement of activities.

—*Activity analysis*: to show the sequence of an event as an activity.[2]

Social network analysis goes beyond the link analysis approach to illustrate and analyze networking. The difference here is not just the difference between a static noun and an active verb. The difference is that network analysis seeks to find, in a wide variety of social relationships and interactions, patterns of causation and explanation (Marsden, 1983; Burt and Minor, 1983). Among some of the various analytical issues of networking are group cohesion, social distance measures, clique patterns, proximity and proximity flows, network density and centrality, influence patterns, and affective and instrumental associational ties. As strategic and tactical intelligence analyses differ, so too the social network or networking approach is similarly different from the link analysis.

I do not wish to make much of these differences, for essentially the goals are the same: understanding. Networking by stressing process and cause simply seeks to focus on a dynamic process rather than a static one.

The Experiment

For a number of years I have wanted to engage in a detailed empirical analysis of the structure, process, and interactions of a major organized crime group or "family" but did not have a sufficient data base for a full empirical study. In 1980, however, I received a data set from individuals in New York City who were familiar with my work and interests. This data set apparently no longer had any current usefulness to the department and may well have been headed for the shredder. It consisted of biographical information collected by law enforcement on the top 100 narcotics violators in the New York City area in the middle and late 1970s. Such information is often commonly referred to as rap-sheet data.

Working through them I became aware of some references to an organized crime group known as "The New Purple Gang." In the data set four known members of the New Purple Gang were listed, along with ten individuals who were listed as suppliers in various degrees of magnitude: (a) major source, (b) source, and (c) possible or "alleged" source.

Sitting in New Mexico 2,000 miles from the scene of the events, I decided that it would be useful to conduct several experiments with this data set. First, the data could be used to see how far one can go in developing an empirical analysis of a crime group from a single, limited source. Second, it could be an interesting test of academic approaches to intelligence analysis, compared with law enforcement methodologies. Third, it would be an opportunity to attempt a computerized social network analysis of a crime group.

From the work that has been done on organized crime groups and their enterprises it is possible to develop a number of analytical propositions about them. Trust, for example, is one of the most basic variables in all interaction. It is even more important in criminal operations, where secrecy, coordination, and interdependence are essential and the costs of exposure are severe. Thus, any network analysis of an organized crime group should seek to understand and evaluate the role of cohesion variables in forming the trust-bonding of the group. In practical law enforcement terms, knowing where the trust bonds and cohesion networks of the group are weak is useful intelligence to any vulnerability analysis. From such studies, targeting of group members who are more vulnerable to becoming informants can be accomplished with both greater accuracy and lower costs.

A review of the literature on organized crime suggests the following cohesion variables are of use in doing social network analysis.

COHESION VARIABLES

—Primary group blood ties and relationships
—Marriage-adoption, extended family ties
—Ethnicity
—Race
—Peer group, age cohort groupings
—Neighborhood-residential proximity (socialization cohorts)
—Educational, fraternal cohorts (especially in white-collar crime)
—Military cohorts (espcially in Black, Anglo, Cuban
   drug-trafficking
   enterprises)
—Prison cohorts (especially Black, Anglo, and motorcycle gangs)
—Nationality (especially Israeli, Colombian, Syrian-Lebanese)
—Parental organized crime ties and history (LCN, Yakusa)
—Language or dialect group
—Religious-territorial (IRA, PLO, Croatian,Armenian terrorist
   groups)
—Expertise Associational (WC crime, mob lawyer-corrupters)
—Interaction frequency and regularity
—Interaction proximity (place)
—Business, crime matrix, or enterprise interdependency
—Mutual interaction dependence (crime skill, profit needs)
—Affective linkages (friendship, attraction)

While this list could be extended, it provides a useful conceptual basis of what helps hold crime groups together. Taking these theoretical variables and using what empirical indicators or variables can be derived from the biographical data sheets, one can create a conceptual focus for the analysis. Allen Dulles once said, "The role of intelligence is to make a lot out of a little." This data set provides an opportunity to illustrate the truth of this view.

The Data Set

The data set contains a number of pieces of information that can be viewed, either directly or indirectly, as cohesion variables. These information bits and their usefulness in a network analysis are presented in Table 4.1.

Given that this research was carried out with little substantive or on-site information, variable 15 became more vital than it would have been had this work been carried out within a law enforcement context. For many organized crime groups, such as motorcycle gangs, data such as past military association, club, prison gang associations, unless present by happenstance in variable 15, would have to be collected elsewhere.

It was from variable 15 that information such as "known member," "leader," along with information regarding "known associate," "source," "major supplier," and "alleged supplier" were obtained. It is important to reinforce that this is a secondary analysis of data gathered for other purposes. I had to accept these labels of rank membership and structural linkage as "true fact." The analysis suggests, however, that at times they should not be labeled as such. Indeed, it suggests that law enforcement intelligence collection techniques could be improved with little cost increase through the use of social network methodologies. There are instances, for example, where the analysis indicates that the street methodologies used by law enforcement may not be providing accurate information.

A second important point to note is that in secondary source analysis, definitions of terms need to be clarified and substantiated. Some facts, such as date of birth, are fairly straightforward. But anyone who has spent time doing actual intelligence analysis for law enforcement on organized crime cases knows that organized criminals often lie about their age. However, they usually shift days and months, and when they change years, it is only by one or two.[3] Thus an age cohort analysis would not be unduly affected by such untruths. But the point remains that when using law enforcement data, or using terms like "associates,"

**TABLE 4.1   Variables in Biographical Data Sheets
Useful in Network Analysis**

Variables	Theoretical Use in Networking
Var. 1. Name	Unit of analysis: the individual
Var. 2. Date of birth (DOB)	Age; age cohort cohesion
Var. 3. Race	Associational cohesion
Var. 3a Ethnicity*	Associational cohesion
Var. 4. Social Security (SS) No.	Socialization proximity (first SS geographic locator)
Var. 5. Residences	Proximity—neighborhood ties
Var. 6. Name, car registration ("owner")	Associational ties
Var. 7. Associates	Associational ties
Var. 8. Areas frequented	Location (area) associational reinforcer
Var. 9. Criminal employment	Skill, crime enterprise ties
Var. 10. Employment	Geographic-skill locator, assoicational reinforcer
Var. 11. Other assets	Locational-associational reinforcer
Var. 12. Family et al.	Primary group, blood, marriage cohesion ties; also crime family ties
Var. 13. Previous residence	Socialization, proximity cohorts
Var. 14. Major case involvement	Crime matrix, associational ties
Var. 15. Background and miscellaneous information	Important structural, rank, position, areal, and other dependent variable information

*The important variable of ethnicity is only directly available in this data set, by name, nickname, spelling, or other family or background information data.

how does the outside analyst evaluate the validity and reliability of these statements? This is obviously a critical problem in secondary analysis, and vitally so in a social network study.

In this particular study, several phone calls to the New York City Police Department Intelligence Unit revealed that this particular department—and, it is hoped, most state and local law enforcement agencies—have a specific and standardized definition of the term "associate." The associate (let us call him A) had to be seen with the subject of the biographical sheet on at least a minimum of three occasions in a regular and lengthy interaction, and observed in this interaction by a sworn officer of the NYPD. This is still not the rigor a social scientist would demand, but it does eliminate casual interactions and informant information or indirect hearsay. The purpose of these individual biographical data sheets is the collection of information about specific individuals and not the New Purple Gang as a group. The high number of reciprocal patterns of association and interaction found (in tables and analyses) suggests that a fairly high level of reliability can be given to this aspect of biographical information. There are, however, other warnings and caveats about this secondary analysis that must be placed before the reader.

Caveat #1: The completeness of this data set is unknown. Completeness can be assumed, but as the analysis suggests, this would likely be an error.

Caveat #2: The identification of "members," "alleged members," and the like is assumed to be incomplete. Later analysis supports this.

Caveat #3: The definition of associate, and the listing thereof, is incomplete.

Caveat #4: The assumption that all individuals cited are in some way actively involved in organized criminal activity involving narcotics trafficking is based solely on their appearance on these biographical data sheets. Almost 100 percent of these individuals have arrest records, but I make no assumption of guilt based on this or on the appearance of an individual's name on these records.

Caveat #5: The purpose of the following analysis is to increase our understanding and knowledge about patterns of association and interaction among individuals who are viewed by law enforcement as engaged in organized crime, and to examine the reliability of certain law enforcement methodologies for their reliability and accuracy. I intend no harm or malice toward the individuals cited here. In most cases their association, membership, and convictions as active members of organized criminal enterprises and conspiracies is well known and part of the public record. The pursuit of new knowledge is the important point, for only through such research and evaluation of records can the whole truth and the usefulness of analytical techniques and ways of improving LE methodologies be known. Thus the reader is warned that the names used in the analysis may or may not be real, and any resemblances to real names or persons should be ignored and held harmless in the mind of the reader. All of the other relationships and networks analyzed here are accurate and true within the stated limitations of a secondary analysis and the data set.

The New Purple Gang

The New Purple Gang was a narcotics trafficking group operating in the New York City metropolitan area in the late 1970s. It was considered one of the major distributors of narcotics in northern Manhattan, the Bronx, and Westchester counties specializing in both heroin and cocaine.

The New Purple Gang is of interest to the organized crime analyst because it not only was an extremely successful drug trafficking group, but was also a third-generation Italian-American crime group with blood ties and relationships to earlier generations of La Cosa Nostra members and associates in the New York area. As such it can provide insights into theoretical propositions regarding ethnic succession and the evolving nature of organized crime. As empirical data regarding these issues is often difficult to obtain, the New Purple Gang, by providing an empirical test of such theories, takes on additional importance and interest.

The New Purple Gang had its roots in the East Harlem neighborhood of New York City's borough of Manhattan (see Figure 4.1). This ten-by-four city block neighborhood has been a traditional home for Italian-Americans, including La Cosa Nostra criminals. At the turn of the century, Ignazio Saietta (Lupo the Wolf) and his brother-in-law, Guiseppe Morello, organized an Italian counterfeiting ring here. Ciro Terranova, a half-brother of the Morellos, rose to prominence as the "Artichoke King" by creating a monopoly over the sale and distribution of artichokes in the city. This racket long predated Jonathan Kwitny's (1979) studies of the "Mafia in the marketplace" and is an early example of business penetration and takeover by organized crime. Joseph Valachi grew up in this neighborhood and began his organized crime career here. So did Carmine Galante, who was born here. East Harlem has been a center for organized crime with a history that long predates Prohibition. It was here that the key leaders of the New Purple Gang were born and raised (see detailed neighborhood map, Figure 4.2).

Examination of the New Purple Gang casts empirical light on ethnic succession theories. The group, although centered among Italian-Americans, worked with both Black and Puerto Rican crime groups in Northern Manhattan and the South Bronx. Just as Charles Luciano and Frank Costello had ties to Irish and Jewish Prohibition criminals, the New Purple Gang had ties to the new ethnics in crime. This gang's openness, like Luciano's, appears to be another step in the Americanization of organized crime.

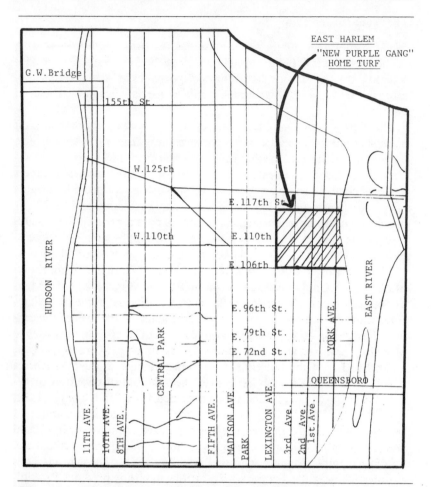

Figure 4.1   Map of Manhattan Island Showing the East Harlem Neighborhood Where the New Purple Gang Has Its Roots

NOTE: See Figure 4.2 for detail of the neighborhood.

Analysis

Following the intelligence dicta of making a lot out of very little, all of the associates of the four "known members" were entered into the computer. This enlarged the possible parameters of the New Purple Gang to some 41 possible members. It seemed unwise, however,

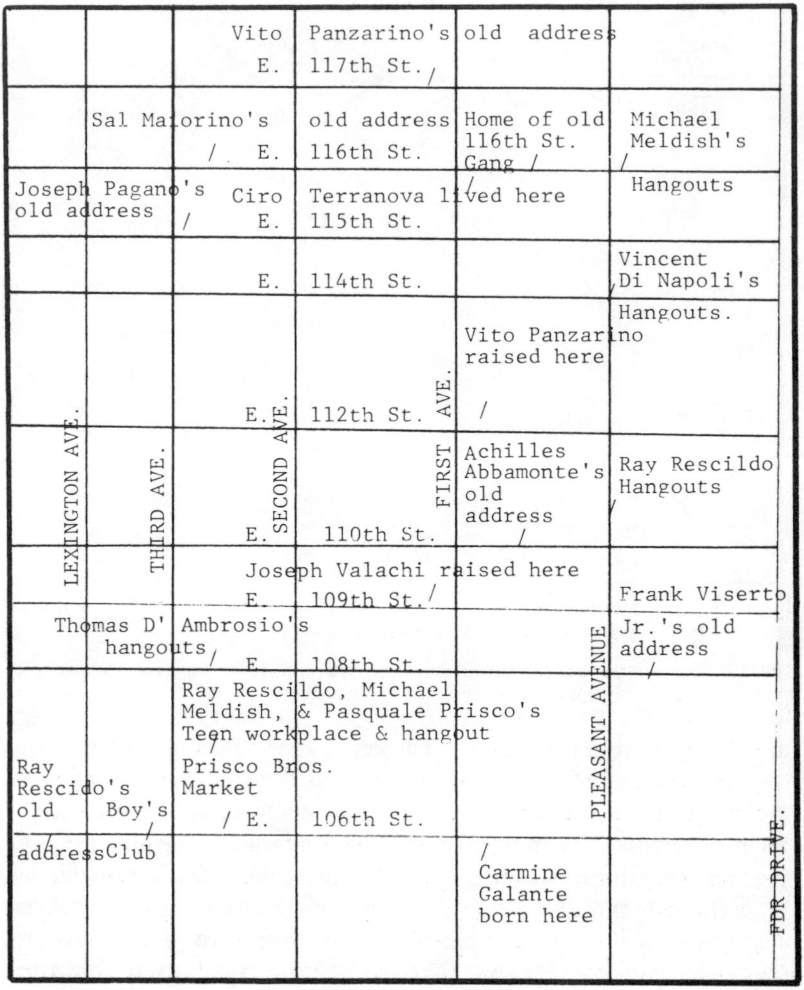

Lexington Ave.	Third Ave.	Second Ave.	First Ave.	Pleasant Avenue	FDR Drive
		Vito E. Panzarino's 117th St.	old address		
	Sal Ma[j]orino's / E.		old address 116th St.	Home of old 116th St. Gang /	Michael Meldish's /
Joseph Pagano's old address		Ciro / E.	Terranova lived here 115th St.		Hangouts
		E.	114th St.		Vincent Di Napoli's
				Vito Panzarino raised here /	Hangouts.
		E.	112th St.		
		E.	110th St.	Achilles Abbamonte's old address /	Ray Rescildo Hangouts /
		Joseph Valachi raised here E.	109th St. /		Frank Viserto
Thomas D'Ambrosio's hangouts / E.			108th St.		Jr.'s old address /
		Ray Rescildo, Michael Meldish, & Pasquale Prisco's Teen workplace & hangout. Prisco Bros. Market / E.	106th St.		
Ray Rescido's old	Boy's			/ Carmine Galante born here	
address	Club				

Figure 4.2 Pleasant Avenue Neighborhood and Roots of the New Purple Gang Members and Associates

simply to accept such a simple-minded conclusion. Thus, any individual who was listed as an associate by one known member but no other member was considered too weak in association to be a gang member

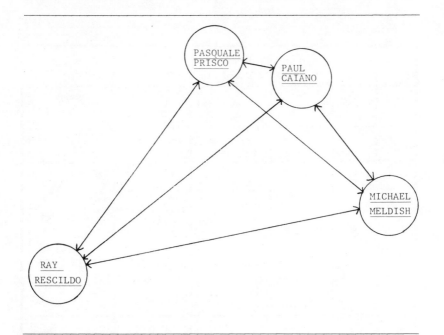

Figure 4.3   Four Known Members of the New Purple Gang According to the Biographical Data Sheets

NOTE: The pattern of association linkages creates a 100% reciprocal network of association and provides confirmation of the data sheets.

and dropped from the analysis. The key to likely gang membership was the strength of the reciprocal ties. Just as the four known members reciprocated ties, according to law enforcement, so the greater the reciprocated ties, the more probable that one was a gang member. The problem, of course, was that data from these individuals were missing from the set—there were only the data from the four known members. Therefore, in a forced compromise, if all four were said to have ties to a given associate, that was taken to indicate fairly strong confirmation of probable membership; three out of four (75 per cent), a weaker support, and two out of four (50 per cent) an even weaker linkage. Given the basic limits of the data, I accepted the 50 percent rule, eliminating only all single mention, nonreinforced statements of association by law enforcement. Figure 4.4 presents these data on the gang. Three or more arrowheads touching a circle suggests probable key members; two arrowheads, likely relevant members or associates. Later analysis will

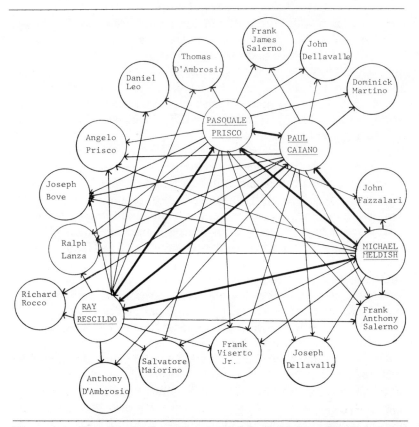

Figure 4.4   New Purple Gang Known and Probable Key Members Based on Network Analysis of Biographical Data Sheets

show that this turned out to be a useful supposition, and the apparent satellites in Figure 4.4 turn out to fit into functional subsets, such as heroin supply and distribution, versus primarily cocaine-marijuana supply and distribution functions.

Cohesion in the New Purple Gang

At this stage of the analysis we are still constructing networks, not engaging in true social network analysis, although the analytical intervention and elimination of some 18 individuals that the link analysis of a law enforcement agency would have included has moved us beyond link analysis. It has also done two more important things. First, it has improved the quality of our criminal targets by eliminating the most peripheral ones, thus in an actual investigation saving time and money. Second, it has removed and probably protected some likely naive, or only tangentially aware citizens, from the microscope of the analyst and thus avoided any inadvertent abuse or infringement of their rights. Unfortunately, the methods we are using here are academic, not real world, but they do suggest the potential improved methodological rigor in actual law enforcement analysis.

To move toward networking, we must look to likely causation of these patterns as well as their associational coherence. The most basic network for social cohesion and trust is blood tie. Family, immediate kinship group, and kinship through marriage create bonds of loyalty that are vital to any successful, ongoing organized crime group.

Among the members of the New Purple Gang such bonds of social cohesion are very important to the functioning of the group. Of the four known members, two are cousins, and two are related by marriage. Extending this to probable key members of the gang, we find three more sets of brothers, and a cross-generational tie between an uncle who is a supplier. Thus, the traditional organized crime tie of blood plays a role in this third-generational Italian-American organized crime group. Figure 4.5 presents the data.

Among the known members, another factor of gang cohesion is age. If one defines an age cohort as someone who shares the same generational history, cultural time references, and the like (as measured for individuals in their 20s and 30s) by five or less years difference in age, all four of the key known members are age cohorts, as in one alleged source of supply. The oldest known member was born in 1946 and the youngest in 1951. If the biographical data were avalable for other individuals I have listed in Figure 4.4 as "probable" New Purple Gang members, many more age cohorts of the post World War II baby boom would likely be found.

A third facet of cohesion among the four known members in addition to age is similar generational socialization; associational cohesion through neighborhood proximity. The neighborhood proximity variable in organized crime group studies is frequently neglected by researchers, but it is an important variable. The Pleasant Avenue neighborhood (shown on the detailed map, Figure 4.2) has been a place of socialization for Italian-American organized criminals since the turn of the century. Three of the known members and seven of their ten alleged suppliers all come from this neighborhood. The New Purple Gang, in

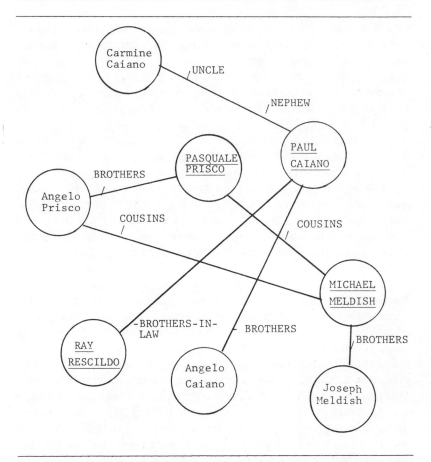

Figure 4.5 Network of Blood Ties and Social Relationship among Known Members of the New Purple Gang

neighborhood terms, is only a step away from the old 107th Street Gang to which Valachi belonged before joining Terranova's 116th Street Gang (Maas, 1969: 57-71). This gang is also only footsteps away from Pleasant Avenue, where other Italian-American crime group figures participated in the drug trade (Durk, 1973).

This history of a neighborhood, a few square blocks, that has been a breeding ground for Italian-American organized crime for over 60 years casts some empirical shadows on the queer ladder theory. There is support for ethnic succession, in that many members of the New Purple Gang, and their suppliers, have moved to the suburbs of the Bronx and Westchester. They are now, like so many New York suburbanite businessmen, commuters to the old neighborhood for work, money, and visiting rather than residents.

The Pleasant Avenue neighborhood is not the only Italian-American neighborhood that appears to possess cross-generational continuity and ties to organized crime. The First Ward in Chicago, Illinois was described in 1909 as being a center of the Black Hand and "Mafia," and in 1982 is still the center, according to the *Chicago Tribune* and Chicago Crime Commission of "Mob" political corruption in the city.[4]

Joseph Albini's (1971: esp. 156-258) work stresses the patron-client ties as a basis of cohesion for organized crime groups. As the "leadership" (i.e., four known members) are all age cohorts, the intergenerational patron-client respect tie is not apparent, though it is likely present. Certainly the ethnic linkages are there, although they may require some clarification for the reader. Some of the four known members have obvious Italian names. Others — Meldish, for example — is an Irish-Italian-American mix (his mother is a Prisco). Ray Rescildo is a Puerto Rican-Italian-American mix (his mother's name is Annunziato). Thus, rather than dealing with pure-blooded organized crime groups of Sicilians, or Calabirians of the 1910s and 1920s, the New Purple Gang is the continuing evolution of organized crime.

For their start-up monies, it is likely that the New Purple Gang was dependent on the older generation of Italian-American criminals to provide financing, while the "kids" took the risks. A number of the known and probable members of the New Purple Gang have either primary group or marriage ties to known, or alleged, La Cosa Nostra members and associates. This reinforces Albini's view of patron-client ties, but more and better empirical data are needed for a true test of his theory. At the same time, this continued intergenerational Italian-American involvement in drug trafficking raises one's doubts about the queer ladder thesis.

Social Networks: The Gang and Its Suppliers

The biographical data sheets list (Variable 15) statements about ten individuals who are said to be suppliers of narcotics to the New Purple Gang. These can be used as labels for them and their alleged activities with the gang. The labels can, in turn, be ordered along a crude ordinal scale. According to the data set, three individuals are "major sources of supply," one individual is "considered a major source of supply"; two are listed simply as "source of supply," and four persons fall under a variety of looser labels: "believed source," "considered a source" "alleged to be . . .," or "possible source." Based on the assumption that language and the strength of expression have meaning, I ranked these individuals and gave them arbitrary weights to separate the apparent, more important suppliers from the more dubious ones (see Table 4.2).

If this information on the biographical data sheets is accurate, one would expect that this experiment in networking would show it. One would expect, for example, that if one is a major supplier, then he would be likely to have denser and tighter associational ties to the New Purple Gang's four known members than, say, a minor supplier. Figure 4.3 presents the data.

This figure, when compared with Table 4.2, raises some questions about the accuracy of the law enforcement labels regarding these suppliers. Figure 4.3 indicates that of the ten individuals who are said to supply heroin and cocaine to the New Purple Gang, 60 percent (6) do not have any reciprocal ties to the four known members of the gang. This could mean (a) that the four known members listed among the 100 most important narcotics violators in New York City in this period were not as important as some other New Purple Gang members who did not make this hit parade, or (b) that if they did make the top 100, they were not recognized as a member of the New Purple Gang, or (c) that law enforcement intelligence misread their relative relationship to the gang. Given the limitations of the data set, can network analysis suggest any answers to these important questions?

Indeed, it can provide a number of nontrivial insights, even given the limits of the data, to where law enforcement intelligence methodologies may have gone wrong. In Table 4.2 the ten suppliers were listed by rank and weight. The higher the weight (4 down to 1), supposedly the more major and important the supplier was to the New Purple Gang. Later the questions can be raised as a hypothesis; that the higher the weight, the more likely to have reciprocal ties with the gang. Figure 4.3 provides us with an estimate of the accuracy of the biographical data (by simply multiplying these weights and reciprocal ties) in terms of this hypothesis.

Table 4.3 shows us that of the three heavyweight suppliers only one has reciprocal ties, while two of the lowest weighted "believed" and "possible" suppliers, according to this network analysis, should be called heavyweights at least in terms of their reciprocal associational ties to the New Purple Gang members.

TABLE 4.2   Suppliers of the New Purple Gang by Rank and Weight

RANK 1.	"A Major Source of Supply"	(Wt. 4)

Achilles Abbamonte
Thomas D'Ambrosio
Vincent Di Napoli

RANK 2.	"Considered a Major Source of Supply"	(Wt. 3)

Carmine Caiano

RANK 3.	"A Source of Supply"	

Martin de Saverio
Vincent Martino

RANK 4.	"Believed" . . . "Considered" . . . "Possible" . . . "Aleged to be . . ."	

	"A Source of Supply"	(Wt. 1)

Salvatore Maiorino
Joseph Pagano
Carmelo Sansone
Frank Viserto, Jr.

**TABLE 4.3   Network Analysis of Suppliers by Linkages
and Rank Weights to New Purple Gang***

Supplier's Name	Weight Rank	X	Reciprocal Linkage	=	Estimate of Bio Sheet Accuracy
Frank Viserto, Jr.	1	X	4	=	4
Thomas D'Ambrosio	4	X	2	=	8
Salvatore Maiorino	1	X	4	=	4
Achilles Abbamonte	4	X	–	=	0
Joseph Pagano	1	X	0	=	0
Carmine Caiano	3	X	1	=	3
Martin de Saverio	1	X	0	=	0
Vincent de Napoli	4	X	0	=	0
Vincent Martino	2	X	0	=	0
Carmelo Sansone	1	X	0	=	0

*Manipulation: weight rank times reciprocal linkages.

TABLE 4.4   Network Analysis Summary of Data Sheet
             Accuracy Regarding Suppliers

Name of Supplier	Estimate of Data Sheet Accuracy (in terms of network analysis)
Thomas D'Ambrosio	Very High
Joseph Pagano	High
Carmelo Sansone	High
Salvatore Maiorino	Fair to Poor
Carmine Caiano	Fair to Poor
Frank Viserto, Jr.	Fair to Poor
Martin de Saverio	Poor
Vincent Martino	Poor
Achilles Abbamonte	Poor
Vincent Di Napoli	Poor

On the reverse side of the coin, the question must be asked why law enforcement methodologies apparently were so far off-base on some 60-70 percent of the group. Table 4.4 compares the bio sheet data with the social network data.

A clue to the inaccuracy of the biographical data sheets can be found by examining Figures 4.6, 4.7, and 4.8. Law enforcement intelligence proved most accurate regarding Thomas D'Ambrosio (Figure 4.7). Comparing this with Figures 4.6 and 4.8, as well as the overall probable group chart (Figure 4.4), one sees how his subnet differs from the other two. Most noticeable is that Paul Caiano and Frank Viserto, Jr. are missing from the D'Ambrosio net. This likely ties to the fact that D'Ambrosio is a heroin supplier, while Mairino and Viserto, Jr. specialize more in cocaine. Indeed, the Viserto, Jr. chart matches the overall group chart (Figure 4.4) so closely that it is likely he is much more than "alleged source of supply"; he is most likely a member of the gang. Given the similarities of the three charts, one explanation of LE error in these three charts, which all show strong ties to the New Purple Gang while intelligence comments hint that only D'Ambrosio is a major supplier, is that law enforcement intelligence must have based their conclusions on some other, different variable.

Checking the neighborhood proximity variable (see detailed map) based on the fact that street experience tells us that big-city narcotics officers spend a lot of time in moving automobile surveillances, we find

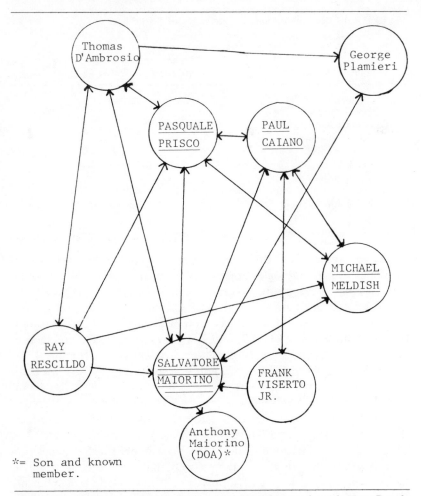

Figure 4.6   Salvatore Maiorino's Associational Network with New Purple Gang Members

NOTE: Similarities and differences exist with D'Ambrosio's network. Double-headed arrows appear to confirm that Maiorino is a cocaine supplier.

the likely root of the intelligence weakness. The map shows that all three of the law enforcement "major sources" either live, have lived, or hang out in proximity to where known members of the New Purple Gang work or hang out. Thus, a rolling automobile surveillance could have

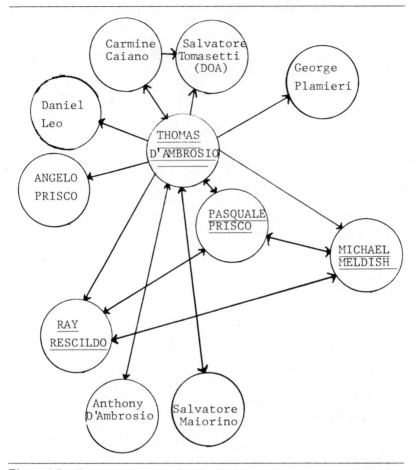

Figure 4.7   Thomas D'Ambrosio's Network: Confirmation of Supplier Status

NOTE: The absence of Paul Caiano from this network supports data that D'Ambrosio is a major heroin supplier while Caiano supplies cocaine. This figure also indicates that structural differences exist between the cocaine and heroin enterprises with a drug trafficking crime matrix.

sighted interactions and quite probably reached the conclusion that these contacts indicated that these suppliers were the gang's major sources of supply. Very different conclusions would have been reached by these law enforcement analysts from a social network analysis, which would

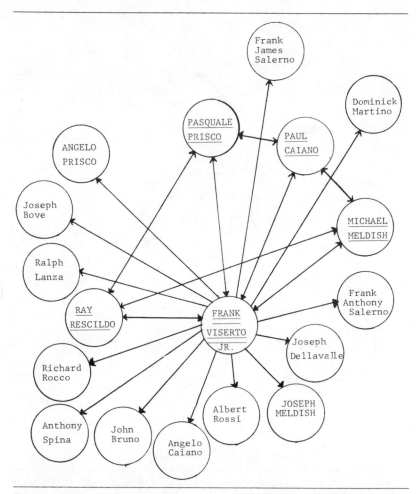

Figure 4.8 Frank Viserto's Network: Independent Confirmation of Key Membership and Supplier Role in the New Purple Gang

NOTE: Viserto's linkages and associations as well as major likely supplier role is confirmed here. This is new knowledge going beyond data sheets.

have shown that this was probably an error and any further investigative time, gas, money, and manpower spent on developing these leads was wasteful and inefficient.

Examining the hangout data (areas frequented variable 8), one finds that both Frank Viserto, Jr. and Pasquale Prisco hang out in the Capri Lounge and Chateau Pelham, thus reinforcing their associational ties, while Pasquale Prisco and Ray Rescildo hang out at the "Seprete Tables," as does "alleged" supplier Martin de Saviero. A sitting surveillance in this lounge could have placed all of them there at the same time on a number of occasions, leading to the conclusion that de Saviero was a supplier, when again the associational network analysis reveals few linkages.

The most fascinating finding, however, is produced by running a cross-generational comparative age cohort analysis on both the suppliers and the known members of the New Purple Gang (Figure 4.9). By constructing this analysis one sees that for those suppliers whom law enforcement intelligence thought were heavyweights but who had no close social network ties to the New Purple Gang, there is more than a decade in age between the gang members and the suppliers. However, those suppliers who have strong social network ties to the gang also have close age cohort ties: Frank Viserto, Jr. is an age cohort, while Thomas D'Ambrosio is less than four or more years' age cohort distance from the known members of the group.

Oddly, at first glance the two other suppliers with solid ties to the New Purple Gang stand some three full decades in age-cohort distance from the group. One piece of information provides a clue to unraveling this apparent peculiarity.

Salvatore Maiorino's biographical data sheet indicates he had a son, Anthony, who was an associate of the New Purple Gang and was a DOA homicide. Looking through Achilles Abbamonte's sheet, one finds mention of one Oreste Abbamonte, but there is no indication if he is a son, brother, or other relative. The age cohort analysis, however, reveals that while these two suppliers are definitely not age cohorts, they are in exactly the proper age cohort group to be fathers of members of the New Purple Gang and their associates. Thus, age cohort analysis tied to social network associational analysis leads us to a possible explanatory proposition about the New Purple Gang. This explanation, while in need of additional data corroboration, appears to be as strongly grounded in fact as the conclusions of law enforcement street intelligence collection methodologies. Thus, these cross-generational associational ties also provide us with empirical support of Albini's patron-client thesis—namely, that the fathers (patrons) supply while the sons (clients) distribute.

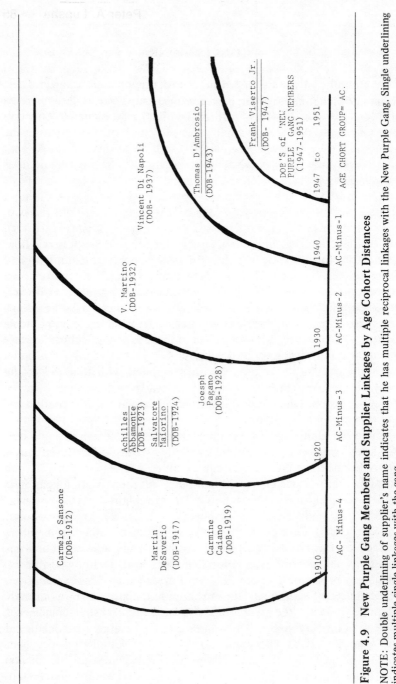

Figure 4.9 New Purple Gang Members and Supplier Linkages by Age Cohort Distances

NOTE: Double underlining of supplier's name indicates that he has multiple reciprocal linkages with the New Purple Gang. Single underlining indicates multiple single linkages with the gang.

CONCLUSIONS

In this study I have engaged in an experiment to examine and test what knowledge about an organized crime group could be gleaned from examination of a single law enforcement data set designed to only collect nominal data on individual subjects. This experiment shows the usefulness of social network analysis as a law enforcement tool. With additional data—or, better, used in conjunction with other methods and active law enforcement cooperation—more hypotheses could be tested.

What we have in this study is a snapshot of an organized crime group, taken with a telephoto lens, a limited f-stop opening, and shot far from the scene of the action. If snapshots such as this could be taken close up with good lighting (i.e., complete data) every three months or so for a period of two or three years, an analytical moving picture of the dynamic social networks of the group could be recorded. Such over-time analysis would capture changing patterns of relationship. Such a series of portraits tied to other intelligence collection techniques— electronic surveillance, informant and undercover methodologies— would result in a rich and detailed tapestry from which both better understanding of organized crime and more efficient methods of interdiction could be developed.

Such analysis would not only improve the quality of prosecution and evidence development, it would lower investigative costs by eliminating less productive investigatory targets and weak leads, and should save innocent or tangentially involved citizens from being directly caught up in the investigation.

This study has also attempted, when possible, to test empirically some of the armchair propositions about organized crime. Its finding casts doubt on Bell's queer ladder thesis. The study also exposes as complete nonsense the beliefs stated by Fratianno and other self-serving literary Italian-American criminals that La Cosa Nostra members and their associates stay away from the drug trafficking crime matrix (Demaris, 1981).[5] This study provides some support for the ethnic succession thesis and the continued evolution of Italian-American organized crime groups. It also provides direct support of the importance of patron-client ties in successful organized criminal enterprise, especially where more tradition-oriented crime groups are concerned.

Finally, this study shows that academic perspectives and methods can assist law enforcement in developing an increased empirical understanding of organized crime groups and their interaction networks. The

academic world can play an important role in separating the fact from
fancy, myth from reality, regarding organized crime. In the search for
and development of this knowledge, both the academic and law enforcement communities can be better served if they would seek to work
and cooperate to develop improved strategic and tactical intelligence,
analytical methods, and techniques.

NOTES

1. Recently the FBI under the leadership of the Social Security Administration. Virgil
Young, of the organized crime division, has begun to undertake this computerized approach. Also see Davis's article on social network analysis (1981).
2. Available from the author on request (*Introduction to Analytical Investigations* hand-
book for ANACAPA Inc. Training Institutes).
3. My experience in doing analysis on organized crime for the New Mexico Gover-
nor's Organized Crime Prevention Commission has shown that a number of organized
criminals lie in giving arrest data about their date of birth; very few, for some reason,
lie on social security number. Corroboration of both data should become standard practice.
4. See Reports of the Chicago Vice Commission, 1906-1909; also later references by
streets and neighborhood names in Kobler (1971) and Landesco (1968). For examples
in the recent period, see *Chicago Tribune*, especially "Police Commission Appointees
and Jane Byrne's Office" series in the fall of 1981.
5. At no point does Fratianno admit drug trafficking connections or experiences in
the LA (Dragna) group. Instead, he states the same old lies that La Cosa Nostra types
"don't touch the stuff." The use of automobile agencies owned by the Dragna group
to import heroin in auto shipments from Japan is a matter of both DEA and FBI investigative records. Similar denials surround the members of the Bruno (Philadelphia)
group and have been exposed as falsehoods.

REFERENCES

ALBINI, J. (1971) The American Mafia: Genesis of a Legend. New York: Appleton-
Century-Crofts.
ANDERSON, A. (1979) The Business of Organized Crime. Stanford: Hoover Institu-
tion Press.
BELL, D. (1953) "Crime as an American way of life." Antioch Review 13 (Summer):
131-154.
BURT, R. and M. MINOR (1983) Applied Network Analysis: A Methodological Introduc-
tion. Beverly Hills, CA: Sage.
CHAMBLISS, W. J. (1978) On the Take. Bloomington: University of Indiana Press.
———and A. BLOCK (1981) Organizing Crime. New York: Elsevier.
CRESSEY, D. (1969) Theft of the Nation. New York: Harper & Row.
DAVIS, R. (1981) "Social network analysis: an aid in conspiracy investigations." FBI
Law Enforcement Bulletin (December).
DEMARIS, O. (1981) The Last Mafioso. New York: Times Books.

DURK, D. (1973) The Pleasant Avenue Connection. New York: Harper & Row.

HALLER, M. H. (1971) "Organized crime in urban society." Journal of Social History (Winter).

IANNI, F. A. J. (1978) "Ethnic succession in organized crime," in NILECJ Summary Research Report. Washington, DC.

———(1974) Black Mafia. New York: Simon & Schuster.

———(1972) A Family Business. New York: Russell Sage.

KAPLAN, L. and D. KESSLER (1976) An Economic Analysis of Crime. Springfield, IL: Charles C Thomas.

KOBLER, A. (1971) Capone. New York: Putnam.

KWITNY, J. (1979) Vicious Circles: The Mafia in the Marketplace. New York: W.W. Norton.

LANDESCO, J. (1968) Organized Crime in Chicago (1929). Chicago: University of Chicago Press.

LUKSETICH, W. and M. WHITE (1982) Crime and Public Policy: An Economic Approach. Boston: Little, Brown.

LUPSHA, P. (1980) "Steps toward a strategic analysis of organized crime." The Police Chief (May).

MAAS, P. (1969) The Valachi Papers. New York: Bantam.

MARSDEN, P.V. (1983) Social Structure and Network Analysis. Beverly Hills, CA: Sage.

NELLI, H. (1976) The Business of Crime. Chicago: University of Chicago Press.

QUINNEY, R. (1977) Class, State and Crime. New York: David McKay.

REUTER, P. and J. RUBINSTEIN (1978) "Fact, fancy, and organized crime." The Public Interest 53 (Fall).

———and S. WYNN (1981) "Racketeering in legitimate industries: two case studies." CRISP Monograph. New York (September).

SALERNO, R. and J.S. TOMPKINS (1969) The Crime Confederation. New York: Popular Library.

SIMON, C. and A. WITTE (1982) Beating the System. Boston: Auburn House.

SMITH, D. Jr. (1975) The Mafia Mystique. New York: Basic Books.

Tom Mieczkowski
Wayne State University

5

SYNDICATED CRIME IN
THE CARIBBEAN
A Case Study

The meaning and description of the term "organized crime" has been
problematic for criminologists for many years. In the literature of the
last two decades there has been a continuing controversy concerning
the function, structure, and existence of organized criminal networks,
generally referred to under the rubric "organized crime." These networks correspond to various theoretical conceptions or models offered
as mixed descriptive and explanatory approaches to the phenomena
under scrutiny. When these models compete, or when their concepts
are exclusive of each other, controversy emerges. This controversy is
compounded by the fact that unlike many areas in sociology, organized crime has a topical, journalistic, and electronic literature as well as
an academic one (Galliher and Cain, 1974). This itself is important as
an effect and even a component of these competing models, and is an
extension of the general methodological problems of the study of
criminal deviance. In this chapter I will seek to develop a typology of
these models, and then report a case study that will utilize this typology.

The major arguments concerning organized crime center on the existence, description, and typology of a "mafia," cosa nostra, or any
system of organizational relationships persisting over time and also
meeting a number of general criteria. First, the network is organized
around the provision of illegal goods and services; second, it uses
violence at its own discretion in order to carry out its organizational
aims; finally, it seeks a market monopoly and legal immunity from arrest, prosecution, and incarceration. In general, its operations classically

have centered on the so-called victimless crimes (e.g., prostitution, gambling, drugs, illicit liquor); "services," such as loansharking, arson-for-hire, protection; and some other areas, such as organized, large-scale fraud, illegal marketing, and political corruption. Its use of violence has largely been seen as rational (in the Weberian sense), in that it is used to promote organizational goals. With a great exception made for the popular and journalistic media, murder and violence by organized criminal syndicates is not based on thrills, kicks, or macho ethics, but as the ultimate resort for the enforcement of rules, contracts, and so on. Its use, in effect, parallels that of the state. Furthermore, these organizations are tellic or purposive. They seek to make money; they are economically oriented. Utilitarian motives translated into economic terms are an asumption of virtually every organized crime model. They vary widely, however, in presenting the ways in which this utilitarian basis is expressed and modified by the relevant sociocultural mileus in which they are found.

The basic syndicate models that conflict can be contrasted on several dimensions (Maltz, 1976). One of the most apparent in the literature is the structural versus the process approach to organized crime. The *structuralist view* was the first to gain wide attention and continues as a dominant view in the field (Albini, 1971). It also is frequently presented as the view most widely held by law enforcement officials, the federal government, and a host of panels, bureaucracies, and commissions that have investigated this topic (see the LEAA report of 1967, for example). The structuralists, as a school, have argued that the criminal syndicate is a highly structured network of sustained relationships describable as a bureaucracy, or in bureaucratic terms. It has various bureaucratic dimensions, such as a division of labor, differentiated status and power, channels of communication, and a chain of command. This network is rigid, formalized, and persists beyond the life or participation of members themselves. It is sustained primarily by two components; the first is a collection of normative forces originating in the larger cultural base in which the syndicate is grounded; the second is in the formal rules and procedures (including sanctions) that are incumbent on all participants. As a consequence of the first component, structuralists tend to emphasize ethnic uniformity, common socialization of values, exterior cultural constraints, and extrapersonal forces. In this regard, for instance, organized crime is often presented as an alien cultural composition (i.e., grounded in an nonnative culture) that has been grafted onto another sociocultural system

(Salerno and Tompkins, 1969). As a consequence of the second component, structuralists point to various phenomena that are symptomatic evidence of their rule systems that govern syndicate behavior. Thus, one is referred to the victims of wars, feuds, and disputes that result in assaults, homicides, and other quasi-military activity, which frequently includes body counts and matching of victim for victim. This is most frequent in the news media (Newsweek, 1982).

Another aspect of the structuralists' first component has been the emphasis on the secret nature of these criminal syndicates. Rituals, vows, pledges, ceremonies, and the like have been described and cited as mechanisms of group integration, security, and distinction. From these initiation and solidarity rites come the force behind group protocol as well as the integration and maintenance of the emotive and utilitarian aspects of syndicate life. Also, because of the heightened cultural specificity of clandestine organizations, one ensures ethnic purity. By its very nature a secret society, being reliant on symbols and meanings available only in a particular socio-cultural and linguistic context, amplifies its own purposes—conducting illegal behavior. Thus, we have the legendary "27 families," for example, who find their ethnic ties complementary to their criminal ones. Furthermore, this secret organization can be expressed by conventional organizational techniques (Pace and Styles, 1972). Thus, we find "families" combined under a "commission," and in turn families are the expression of other combinations of units (e.g., soldati or capos). Concomitant with these various structural statuses are rules, regulations, and codes that provide the behavioral component to them. There have been a variety of these provisos described, including the most famous "omerta" or the rule of silence (Gage, 1972).

Beginning with the mid-1960's, a number of studies emerged that challenged the structural position, and in its stead proposed an alternative model of organized crime I will call the "process view." Albini (1969), Hess (1973), Smith (1975), Hawkins (1969), and others have, by a variety of approaches, attacked the structuralist position. It has been attacked as factually inaccurate, as being based more on myths, preconceptions, folklore, and imagination than on actual empirical data. The structual position has been further attacked as being biased, especially in treating identical criminal behaviors as not identical when there are extraneous differences, such as race or ethnicity. The attitude toward criminals is thus altered in a manner consistent with what has been called "labeling theory." Structuralism has also been accused of self-contradiction, tautology, and naivete. This critique of the structuralist approach has been supplemented by another competing point of view, which emphasizes process and interaction between participants as the most fruitful area for the understanding of syndicate crime.

The process view argues that group relation networks labeled "mafia" are best understood as an extension of the generalized interaction and exchange processes inherent in social life. These networks are not rigid and highly formalized; rather, they are plastic, rife with change, and not translatable into the conventional bureaucratic models. Although they endure when using certain measures, they constantly change when the measures change. They are ad hoc, shifting alliances that are negotiated and defined situationally. There is no utterly or absolutely unique quality to the kinds of relationships that are operant in organized criminal syndicates—they are manifestations of the same forces one would find in any utilitarian conglomerations. Thus, the process theorists argue that not only is the image of the rigid structural model with its secretive membership a lacking one, but that it distorts social reality, in that it arbitrarily excludes identical forms of behavior on the basis of meaningless distinctions. Structuralists concentrate on the particular actors as the ultimate unit of analysis; process models concentrate on the acts themselves. For process theorists, organized crime is seen as a relationship system concerned with the exchange of things and is governed by pragmatism and utility that is relevant to the goals of the actors. The criminal syndicate may have its form influenced by particularistic items, but its general forms are explainable by broader, more universal concepts. Thus, syndicate crime is not the exclusive cultural property of any one group, nor is it captured in any particular organizational format. One can find a variety of environments and circumstances that express and nurture syndication and the needs it satisfies in human society.

The distinctions between these two competing models of organized crime are summarized in Table 5.1. The purpose of this chapter is to present the results of a case study in which the two models were applied and the process model seems to offer the better fit of model to data. This study attempts to lend clarification to the ongoing controversy by providing additional data for analysis and evaluation—material based on actual field observation of syndicate activity, which has been rare in the literature. In addition, this is also a cross-cultural study, in which we compare syndicate activity in the Caribbean to that of the United States. Such cross-cultural comparisons on organized crime have likewise been rare.

TABLE 5.1   Comparison of the Structural and Process Models
of Syndicates

| Mechanism | Typology of Syndicate Model | |
	Structuralist	Process
Organization	rigid, bureaucratic, formal	loose, shifting, coalitional
Cohesion	overarching cultural norms and values; values precede utility	utility and pragmatism; utility precedes value
Membership	ethnicity, race, homogeneity of types, esp. ethnicity and race	expediency and propinquity; ethnic and racial heterogeneity
Motivation	group persistence for its own sake; the goal is subordinate to the group	pragmatic achievement of goals; the group is subordinate to the goal

METHODOLOGY

This study is the result of my experience as a participant in a particular social environment in the roles of worker and periodic resident on the island of Trinidad. The information presented here was assembled while I worked as a sailor on small island cargo vessels operating in the Caribbean between 1972 and 1974. This role was a natural or normal one, in that there is a vigorous and ongoing interisland trade using such ships. Likewise, there is an everchanging body of sailors, adventurers, and itinerants of various kinds who supply the manpower to the business. I was among this group—not a native certainly, but nevertheless engaged in a well-accepted and normal role for the social structure. It is important to stress that I did *not* take on this role with the deliberate purpose of gathering data for this study. The value of the experience for sociological purposes was not realized until the experience was well under way. The people and events described were encountered in the normal course of work and life in the islands. The contacts were the result of serendipidity, which after awhile were increasingly supplemented by trying to cultivate relationships that would in fact expand my knowledge on these subjects.

Perhaps this combination of factors is best illustrated by noting how I first came into contact with participants in the syndicate. The first night shore leave was available in Port O'Spain (the capital city of Trinidad/Tobago). I was in the company of a young boy who was a member of the ship's crew. In the course of walking around the city and taking in the sights, this young fellow saw a motorcycle parked in front of a night club. He began to shout "That's Herbert's, that's Herbert's!" It was the motorcycle of a friend that he had seen before. He persuaded me to go into the club to find Herbert (the boy himself was too young to go into the club). Thus I met Herbert, and the first contact was made. From this initial contact came a series of relationships and friendships which constitute in part the data for this study.

The description herein is based on my experience as reconstructed by recollection, notes, diaries, and document research. The information was obtained through experiences and relationships with syndicate members. These experiences occurred in the context of a natural working role in the social structure and were only later "digested" and rendered into a sociological format. This is a variation on what, in sociology, is usually termed participant observation. It is also a sort of social history, or history with a sociological perspective. It is a cruder and less consciously created experience in the spirit of Whyte's *Street Corner Society* or Liebow's *Tally's Corner*. It is offered as a worthwile source of information on organized criminal activity, and as a qualitative study of syndicate operation in the Caribbean. As its basic hypothesis it states that such organized criminal activity as witnessed is best and most accurately understood as a loosely structured network of patron-client relationships.

FINDINGS AND DISCUSSIONS

This study is concerned with an organized criminal syndicate I will call the Ras Boys, a group of age-mixed males born, raised, and living in a particular section of Port O'Spain, Trinidad. The section in which they lived I will call the Bridge district, which is an old, poor, but highly cohesive neighborhood. Although this community was poor in economic terms, it was rich in community spirit and history.

To understand the Ras Boys, it is first necessary to understand something about the community from which they emerged. The people of the Bridge are all "long-time" residents. Mansah, the Ras Boys leader, was born three houses from where he lived during the course of our experiences there. This was the general rule for residents in the community. Futhermore, the people of this community were united by more than proximity, in that they also shared a common history and set of experiences intimately tied into Trinidad's struggle against and liberation from colonialism. Likewise, they shared the experience of Carnival, which in many ways is the broadest and grandest expression of the national sentiments and feelings that bind together the country as a whole, and bind together many communities by their participation in the Carnvial celebration. The Ras Boys syndicate was also bound up in the Carnival cycle and found its early identity, formation, and expression as a group through Carnival participation.

Carnival is, for Trinidadians, a yearly celebration and expression of joy replete with dancing, jumping up, drinking, smoking "ganja" (marijuana), and general unrestrained exuberation. Ostensibly, it is the celebration of "Mardi Gras" or Fat Tuesday, the final fling before Lent. Carnival has a more profound and latent meaning as well. Historically, it has been argued to be a device for the release of the pent-up frustrations, anxieties, and repression of a colonial people, a people with a long history of slavery, oppression, exploitation, and foreign domination. It is a modern reminder of the colonial past, a link with what Trinidad was and is today. One must see Carnival to understand the society. As is true in all sections of the capital city, Carnival is celebrated with great zest and careful preparation by residents of the Bridge. And it is through the participation of the community in the celebration, and the leadership of the Ras Boys in the preparation and carrying out of the celebration, that we first encounter their ties to the community. The Ras Boys syndicate is centrally involved with the Carnival celebration.

The Ras Boys are the primary planners and organizers of the Carnival celebration. They organize and support the local steel band, they produce and supervise the construction of the local float, they design and procure materials for the production of the theme costumes that will be worn by community people who "play mas" that year in the celebration. Likewise they play a major role in securing the rum, ganja, and other intoxicants desired by the community. In this role the Ras Boys stand out as a clear and predominantly legitimate community organization, integrated with the community as a kind of leadership group. This is the result of their initiative in seizing this role; in addition, they are the inheritors of the "jamette" tradition, another historical aspect of Carnival. In brief, the Carnival historically has had an aspect of violence, especially centered in the poor districts of the city. This violence has centered on competition between various neighborhoods or districts. Each district has a distinctive costume, a particular band, and even unique and particular calypsos they write for the Carnival. Groups from different districts clashed, often violently (Pearse,

1956). The level of violence was sometimes quite severe. Status and power within a district came to be awarded on the basis of individual performances in these interdistrict conflicts. The young men of the district were "bad johns" or jamettes and the toughest and fiercest was awarded high status as a result of good performance "in combat." It was as the inheritors of this jamette tradition that the Ras Boys also held and wielded power in the community. They were seen as "warriors" for the community and thus were treated with respect and deference by community members (the Ras Boys were often the settlers of intracommunity disputes), and the experience together of engaging in this role lent strong cohesion to the Ras Boys themselves.

However, the Ras Boys should not be thought of as some sort of public service group. They also were a profit-making criminal syndicate and used their community role to this end as well. They engaged in the provision of illicit goods and services to the local community and beyond. Their enterprises included the provision of marijuana, cocaine, "bush" rum (white lightning), some stolen materials, political patronage jobs, and protection in terms of physical force. Thus, the Ras Boys served two roles and these two roles were intertwined. The legitimate functions blended into the illegitimate ones. Service to the community was in both legitimate and illegitimate domains. They both served and exploited. They had both altruistic and profit-seeking motives; and they were not, in the minds of the Ras Boys, either separate or separable.

The Ras Boys were a criminal syndicate according to the process model of syndication. At the time of this study the Ras Boys were tightly bonded as a group. The syndicate consisted of a core group, the Ras Boys themselves, and some ancillary people who were essential to syndicate operations. The core group lived in and spent their time in the Bridge community, but this was not necessarily true of the ancillary personnel (see Figure 5.1).

Figure 5.1 represents the network of patron-client relationships which constituted the Ras Boys' criminal syndicate. This network was concerned mostly with the distribution of ganja and occasionally with the distribution or transferring of cocaine. Additionally, this group infrequently handled other types of contraband. The most important activity for getting steady income was the distribution and sale of ganja. The marijuana was secured from two sources, either that which was locally grown (and generally considered of inferior quality) and that which was imported from South America, primarily Colombia or Venezuela. Regardless of the origin, the standard distribution practices

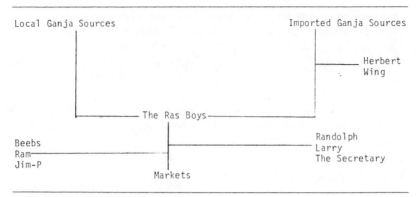

Figure 5.1   The Ras Boys Syndicate

were the same. The marijuana would be delivered to a central warehouse or locale. Large divisions of the contraband would take place first, pound or greater quantities being disbursed to various local wholesalers. The Ras Boys would then take what they had retained for their own retail operation, and by employing street vendors they would roll up hundreds of individual joints or marijuana cigarettes. These joints would then be turned over to the street vendors on consignment, who would then sell ("push" is the term they preferred) on the street for $1 or $1.50 depending on the quality and level of supply. These street vendors enjoyed relative immunity from arrest due to the protection of Randolph, a police officer of rank (see Figure 5.1). Randolph protected the Ras Boys' vendors from arrest as part of a patron-client exchange; Randolph receiving information and some quantities of drugs for personal use for the immunity.

When imported marijuana was sold, it involved the use of a 'fixer,'' whom I call Herbert. Herbert would make the foreign contacts and arrange for the smuggling of the contraband into the Ras Boys' hands. He possessed several invaluable assets that were of use to the syndicate. First, he was a Caucasian. This fact permitted him to move easily in social circles and circumstances that would be "off limits" to blacks, especially the Ras Boys. Second, Herbert was the son of a diplomat, and thus his travel was not considered unusual, and his treatment by various customs and immigration officials was deferential. Herbert also spoke Spanish, and since the sources of imported marijuana were in Spanish-speaking nations, this was an essential skill. It should be noted

that the close cooperation between blacks and whites in syndicate activity was viewed as unlikely by local police and the population in general.
This was a prejudice that the Ras Boys worked to their advantage. In
general, the syndicate was characterized by a greater racial and ethnic
diversity than the rest of Trinidadian society. The Ras Boys, and Mansah in particular, liked to draw attention to this fact.

Another example of this diversity may be seen by examining the role
of Wing, an ethnic Chinese born in Trinidad, who functioned as a
"bank" or capitalizer for contraband purchases. In return for the use
of his money, Wing received some contraband for his personal use or
resale. Additionally, Wing operated several successful businesses in the
community (a bar, a bar-restaurant, and a brothel) which served both
as a source for his cash and as a potential resale market for drugs. Also,
at some of these businesses there was ongoing illegal gambling, which
not only provided additional (and unrecorded) cash for various enterprises, but was also a good drug-selling milieu. At these gambling lo-
cales it was the Ras Boys who provided "security" personnel, ensur-
ing that the games were orderly and that gambling obligations were paid.

Two other individuals were an integral part of the syndicate: One
I call Larry, the other the Secretary. Larry had been raised in the Bridge
community and had made a career in the customs and immigration service. In return for the acquisition of marijuana for personal use and
also because of emotional attachment to the community, Larry was
willing and able to provide information discreetly to the Ras Boys that
would be of importance to their syndicate operations. This information was of obvious value to a syndicate whose greatest concern is smuggling. The Secretary was the least known of all the syndicate operatives;
he was attached to the national government. He was reported to have
access to the highest government officials, including the prime minister.
The Secretary was the ultimate ensurer of arrest immunity for the
highest-ranking members of the syndicate. His relationship to the syndicate was based on an agreement made with the national government
into which the syndicate had entered during the "black power revolu-
tion" that occurred in the early 1970s. During a period of civil unrest
and an abortive coup attempt by a faction of the national defense force
of Trinidad in the early 1970s, the government in power made an active attempt to neutralize potential sources of opposition or revolu-
tionary activity, including the Bridge community and the Ras Boys.
To this end Mansah was approached and asked to use his power to
keep citizens off the street and to discourage looting or any civil unrest
in his community. He consented to the overture, but on the condition

that the government ensure his immunity from arrest in the selling and distribution of marijuana or other forms of minor drug trafficking (note that no "hard" narcotics were involved) and that his domination of a patronage job system (known as the "road gang" system) be continued.

Based on my data, it is evident that the Ras Boys as a group displays many of the important facets of organized criminal syndicates as described by the process perspective. The functional meanings of syndicate activities are complex and multidimensional. The Ras Boys, as one component of the syndicate, had a relationship system that can be interpreted only in a variety of spheres of interests. They were involved, via Carnival, in the open and legitimate activity of the community in which they lived. They functioned in other ways to facilitate legitimate social life in the community as well (e.g. by arbitrating disputes, aiding residents in sundry ways, providing security to the streets of the district, etc.). Likewise, they had quasi-legitimate functions as political patronage dispensers in the road gang system—which involved the dispensation of government-subsidized work that produced some cash for very little if any actual work. The Ras Boys clearly catered to the illegal needs and desires of the community. Contraband, intoxicants, stolen merchandise, and assorted gambling opportunities were some of these services. Their relationship to the community was diffuse, multifaceted, and not without a certain ethical and moral ambiguity.

Did the Ras Boys serve themselves or the community? Did they exploit their environment or serve it? These questions were not relevant to the Ras Boys, especially as abstractions. In their daily perception of events, they would hardly view themselves as exploiters of the very community in which they lived and identified with as residents. Much of their work was for no material gain; its only reward would be in terms of community pride and status. The Ras syndicate could not be described as a rigid organization, as is perceived by the assumptions of the structuralist model, or as a familial, racial, or ethnic organization either. The relationship base on which the syndicate formed was complex, multidimensional, heterogeneous, and essentially utilitarian. Some relationships emphasized such things as shared life experience, common socialization, and emotional ties. Some were clearly expedient, and others unlikely under nonsyndicate conditions. Most were a mixture of expediency, emotion, utility, and rationalization.

Based on these data, it seems untenable to describe this kind of network in bureaucratic terms. Leadership was informal and it was based on personal achievement rather than structural position. Power was relative and not fixed or compartmentalized, nor was it formally administered. Power and status can, in fact, be best described in particularistic terms that are implicit in the process model of organized crime. The most common feature was that the relationship seemed inevitably to involve exchange and that these exchanges were constructed and reconstructed on the basis of perceived and mutually beneficial arrangements among participants.

CONCLUSIONS

In the literature of the past two decades one can find presentations of various models of organized crime along a dimension called structure process. This dichotomy has been demonstrated in the emphasis a theory places on such variables as organizational formality versus informality, the relative stasis of organizational forms versus their flux, the homogeneity of participants along several variables (such as ethnicity, sex, race, etc.) versus the heterogeneity of these factors, and the ad hoc or utilitarian motives of such groups versus kinship, ritual, tradition, norms and other structural motives. In the case of the Ras Boys syndicate, it appears that the process model would be of greater value in describing and interpreting their criminal activity. The social behaviors that have frequently been described as significant to criminal syndicates (e.g., ethnic uniformity, ritual activity, dominance of kinship) are largely absent in this context. In their place we find more immediate forms of exchange of valued entities, both physical and emotional, that may be called patron-client relationships. The group is a means to other ends, and not an end in itself. No single factor seems to run throughout the entire range of the syndicate. Such factors as social propinquity, common socialization, social class, and the like seem to explain various aspects and components of the syndicate. However, none explains a dominant proportion, nor does any appear uniformly in all parts of the syndicate. Variability would be a good term to describe the nature of syndicate relationships:

> The structure of syndicate crime . . . is not confined to a rigidly organized group but rather has relationships drawn from a variety of sources criminal and non-criminal. Its enterprises are generated at all levels of patron-client relationships and they are primarily held together by the fact that each participant is basically motivated by his own self interest (Albini, 1975).

It seems that the process model of syndication, based on the data of this study, is a superior explanatory conception of criminal syndication. More research needs to be done in two basic areas. First, research should rely more on field reporting of actual ongoing criminal syndicates. This requires the penetration of such organizations, and the translation of this endeavor into sociological analysis. Where penetration has been accomplished, it has largely been done by journalists, police investigators, or retired and/or reformed syndicate criminals. Sociologists studying this area have not, for the most part, accomplished this. This kind of research can be dangerous. It involves special skills that are perhaps hard to cultivate and apply. It is also reliant on some degree of serendipity, making it an uncertain research data source. For obvious reasons, sociologists are not often willing to take this risk (Albini, 1981).

Second, more could be done to apply some contemporary quantitative techniques, such as causal modeling theory, to analysis of the organizational formats of syndication. It might be possible to quantify some of the dimensions of these systems and thus lend a new analytic format to their study. Although there are some obvious problems—such as operationalization—it nevertheless seems possible that this may be a productive approach in an area that cries out for new techniques of understanding and evaluation.

REFERENCES

ALBINI, J. (1981) "Reactions to the questioning of the Mafia myth," The Mad, The Bad, and the Different. Lexington, MA: D.C. Heath.

———(1975) "Mafia as method: a comparison between Great Britain and the U.S.A. regarding the existence and structure of organized crime." International Journal of Penology and Criminology, Volume 3.

———(1971) The American Mafia: Genesis of a Legend. New York: Appleton-Century-Crofts.

GAGE, N. [ed.] (1974) Mafia, U.S.A. Chicago: Playboy Press.

GALLIHER, J. and J. CAIN (1974) "Citation support for the Mafia myth in criminology texts". The American Sociologist, Volume 9 (May).

HAWKINS, G. (1969) "God and the Mafia." Public Interest 14 (Winter).

HESS, H. (1973) Mafia and Mafiosi: The Structure of Power. Lexington, MA: D.C. Heath.

Task Force on Organized Crime (1967) Task Force Report: Organized Crime. Washington, DC: Government Printing Office.

MALTZ, M. (1976) "On defining organized crime." Crime and Delinquency, Volume 22, 6.

Newsweek (1981) "How the Mob really works." January 5 1981.

PACE, D. and J. STYLES (1975) Organized Crime. Englewood Cliffs, NJ: Prentice-Hall.

PEARSE, A. (1956) "Carnival in the 19th century." Caribbean Quarterly, Volume 4, 3.

SALERNO, R. and J. TOMPKINS (1969) The Crime Confederation. Garden City, NY: Doubleday.
SMITH, D. (1975) The Mafia Mystique. New York: Basic Books.

Alan A. Block
Frank R. Scarpitti
University of Delaware

6

DEFINING ILLEGAL HAZARDOUS WASTE DISPOSAL
White-Collar or Organized Crime

Among the forms of unlawful behavior assuming new significance in recent years is the illegal disposal of hazardous wastes. In the 1970s, this behavior became more frequent, was identified, legislated against, and subjected to some investigation and prosecution (Wilheim, 1981). These efforts have been only minimally successful, however, since the problem is not diminishing and most illegal dumpers appear to have remained untouched by law enforcement efforts (U.S. House of Representatives, 1981). Perhaps this is partly the result of how the problem has been conceptualized. In this chapter, we shall discuss the manner in which the illegalities of hazardous waste disposal have been presented, and examine the outcome of currently prevalent definitions. Our focus will be on the state of New Jersey because it ranks among the leaders of toxic waste-generating states and because it has an established official governmental apparatus to control the problem.

For the most part, as we shall see, illegal hazardous waste disposal has been placed under the category of white-collar crime. It is also true that the phenomenon is analyzed in numerous law journal articles (Kahan, 1978; Caynor, 1977; Zener, 1977) as another example of in-

AUTHORS' NOTE: We would like to thank Jeremiah McKenna, Jim Poulos, and Gerry Wendelken of the New York State Senate Select Committee on Crime for their generous assistance on this project.

dustrial pollution in general. These essays typically discuss questions dealing with the role, functions, and intent of various regulations and regulators. The analysts question how the state can handle (regulate) what have been called at times the "sleazy" characters who illegally dump hazardous wastes. These, it is assumed, are the numerous operators of small firms that haul hazardous waste from the generators to what are sometimes improper disposal facilities. Moreover, the suggestion runs deep that the dumpers, although acting illegally, are unconnected to any wider historical, sociological, or political context; they are, to put it simply, mobile entrepreneurs of hazardous waste.

It is our contention, on the other hand, that large numbers of these mobile entrepreneurs are career criminals—specifically, organized crime figures (Block and Scarpitti, 1982). Furthermore, we argue that the hazardous waste disposal industry is not just partly made up of career criminals, but that its structure is determined by organized crime syndicates. Therefore, we find that the characterization of the problems associated wth the illegal disposal of hazardous waste as a variant or type of white-collar crime to be incorrect, perhaps even insidious. The point is not whether particular offenses or offenders should be placed in one sociological or criminological schema or another, but rather the manner in which social problems are both conceptualized and contextualized. White-collar offenses suggest not only class and workplace issues, not only particular enforcement and prosecutive strategies, but also a perception of reality. In this case what is most intriguing about the version of reality promoted by those who insist on characterizing hazardous waste dumping as white-collar crime is what is left outside its parameters.

Before proceeding with the main features of the discussion, it should be clear that we are not speaking to the old but significant Sutherland claim that "white-collar crime is organized crime."[1] All students of criminology realize that this is the case in almost all instances of corporate deviance. The distinction we are addressing is not the similarity between known organized crime figures on the one hand and corporate executives on the other. Instead, we are concerned with the political and intellectual ramifications that result from the labeling of certain law violations in a particular way.

THE MANNER OF PRESENTATION: FOCUS ON STIER

Edwin H. Stier was, until the first week of October 1982, director of the Division of Criminal Justice in New Jersey. In this capacity, he directed certain law enforcement efforts within the state dealing with illegal hazardous waste disposal. As director of criminal justice, Stier played a major role in defining types of illegal activities. Not just in establishing investigative and prosecutorial priorities and strategies, but in presentations to various public audiences, the authoritative statements by Stier and others in similar positions are significant.

Perhaps the most complete and interesting written presentation by Stier on illegal hazardous waste disposal was published in the fall of 1980. Contained within the Battelle report entitled *The Development of a Research Agenda on White-Collar Crime* was an article by Stier on "The Interrelationships Among Remedies for White-Collar Criminal Behavior" (1980).

Before focusing on Stier's article, however, it must be pointed out that in the introduction to the volume, Herbert Edelhertz, Director of the Law and Justice Study Center of Battelle, comments wisely on the many confusions surrounding the term "white-collar crime" and what it signifies. Edelhertz writes that "the study of white-collar crime presents unique challenges to those who undertake it. There are problems of definition and of data availability and interpretation" (Edelhertz and Overcast, 1980: 1). Indeed, he adds that white-collar crime research has recently expanded because of "new concerns" with a whole string of criminological issues, not the least of which are "public corruption," the "abuses of power inherent in looting of pension funds," and the "links between white-collar and organized crime" (Edelhertz and Overcast, 1980: 3).

While no typology of white-collar offenses is offered, a quasi-definition does appear: "White-collar crime is in large part crime by, within, among, or against business" (Edelhertz and Overcast, 1980: 8). Although it is not so stated, we may assume that Edelhertz means so-called legitimate businesses as opposed to such businesses as policy banks or syndicate loan-shark operations. Obviously enough, white-collar type offenses, as indicated in the introduction, may exist on some continuum with organized crime or be linked to organized crime in some other fashion. It would even seem quite possible, given the above partial list of expanded research issues, that white-collar crime may be carried out—hypothetically, at least—by career criminals as commonly understood. However, while the logic is clear, it is nonetheless an issue neither specifically addressed nor seriously entertained. Undoubtedly, it is missing because the field of white-collar crime is still primarily confined to organizational concerns and, at most, part-time miscreants.

Therefore, it seems that even as white-collar crime research expands into new arenas, it may well be no less amorphous.

Let us turn now to Stier's article in the Battelle collection. To begin with, he makes it absolutely clear that his topic is white-collar crime, which, he writes, "covers a broad spectrum of illegitimate conduct directed against or arising out of legitimate governmental or commerical activity and consequently falls within the purview of a variety of public and private institutions" (1980: 171). Stier goes on to note that because white-collar crime has such a protean nature, it is extemely difficult to control—or, as he puts it, the "maximization of present potental has not fully materialized and efforts to control economic crime have thus far been relatively unsuccessful" (1980: 171). One of the major claims advanced by Stier for the failure to control is the "fragmentation" of "the existing framework of control" (1980: 172-173).

In order to display both the fragmentation of the control apparatus and to "fully understand those obstacles which presently hinder efforts to effectively combine the most appropriate available remedies and resources to deal with a particular white-collar crime problem"(1980: 180), Stier turns to illegal hazardous waste disposal. He first discloses the magnitude of the problem: In 1977, for instance, the state of New Jersey produced "1.2 billion gallons" of liquid chemical waste and about 350,000 tons of "toxic sludge" of which approximately 90% "was not disposed of in a legitimate or environmentally sound manner" (1980: 180). Next, he describes how the Division of Criminal Justice only inadvertently learned of this problem. Once informed, however, Criminal Justice conducted an investigation and then advised New Jersey's Department of Environmental Protection (DEP) of their findings. This produced the first instance of control fragmentation.

Actually, the initial problem, as Stier notes, was one of perception, with DEP maintaining that illegal hazardous waste dumping was of only "temporary duration, caused by the closing of the state's largest chemical landfill site which until 1975 accepted toxic chemical waste" (1980: 181). Given this perception of the problem, a particular strategy emerged on the part of DEP: It would encourage the fledgling disposal industry "by establishing liberal licensing and inspection standards" (1980: 181) while simultaneously pressuring the Division of Criminal Justice to focus on the "black market of illegal haulers." Stier adds that the presence of the black market was believed by DEP to have come about because "the recycling industry, that is, that part of the industry which has developed the technology to legitimately dispose of toxic chemical waste by breaking it down, incinerating it, etc., was too young to provide a total market for all the generators" (1980: 181), and therefore forced generators to deal with illegal haulers. Clearly enough, DEP, according to Stier, viewed the situation as a market problem; an immature industry which with proper support would fill the gaps then filled by illegal haulers.

Contrary to DEP's perception of the problem and its causes, the Division of Criminal Justice found that illegal toxic waste dumping was not confined to the black market of illegal haulers but reached as well to the disposal facilities themselves. The fledgling industry counted on by DEP was itself engaged in much the same type of criminality as the illegal haulers. Accordingly, Stier's finding placed the Division of Criminal Justice at odds with DEP, with the result that the "impact of criminal law enforcement" was undermined by "the support and protection afforded to licensed companies by the agency charged with their regulation" (1980: 181-182). The apparent problem was most succinctly described by Stier in the following manner:

> The regulatory agency, having decided that the ultimate solution to the toxic waste problem was the rapid development of the recycling industry, tended to overlook signs that the industry was becoming corrupt. The Division of Criminal Justice, on the other hand, which had no responsibility to find a solution to the toxic waste problem but which measured its success in terms of criminal prosecution, suspected that the industry as a whole was dishonest and should not be trusted [1980: 182].

Among the results of this disagreement was the breakdown of communication between the Division of Criminal Justice and DEP. In fact, Stier remarks that a broad range of institutional problems between the regulatory agency and law enforcement erupted; "parochial or jurisdictional pride" was invoked as "each agency was apprehensive of having its internal policies shaped by others" (1980: 182).

The catalogue of problems between the two agencies reported by Stier was not attributable entirely to the differences in perception. Some involved the "incompatible standards" or different "institutional values" that are built into the conflicting agencies. As an example of this situation, Stier offers the following:

> Put another way, if the DEP remains convinced that a recycling company is sincerely attempting to reach the agency's goal of legitimate toxic waste disposal, present violations may be tolerated. It is the percep-

tion of the character of the recycling company not simply the objective facts which will influence the DEP's enforcement attitude. The Division of Criminal Justice, however, is influenced less by the long-term view of the potential role of the subject of investigation in the industry and more by its present behavior [1980: 184].

Obviously, illegal hazardous waste disposal in the state of New Jersey is consistently characterized by Stier, first and foremost, as a white-collar crime and, second, as one highly resistant to law enforcement activities because of conflicting interpretations of the problem and the natural and normal rivalries between law enforcement and regulation. In the remainder of his article Stier addresses certain key institutional changes enacted in New Jersey specifically to coordinate the state's response to the issue of illegal hazardous waste disposal. These changes will be analyzed later, after we consider the cogency of describing illegal hazardous waste disposal as a particular type of white-collar crime.

THE MANNER OF PRESENTATION:
ENVIRONMENTAL CONTROL AND ORGANIZED CRIME

On September 25, 1979 (the year preceding the Battelle publication), Stier presented a somewhat different version of the problems associated with the illegal disposal of hazardous waste (National Association of Attorneys General, 1979). At that time he was addressing a seminar composed of both organized crime enforcement authorities and environmental specialists. During his presentation Stier noted that he did not yet believe that, as he called them, "traditional, Mafia-type elements of organized crime" have established direct control over the hazardous waste industry. He immediately pointed out, nevertheless, that "organized crime dominates" the solid waste industry in New Jersey, and he added that the Division of Criminal Justice, which had been investigating the solid waste industry, now recognized "that some of the companies involved in solid waste disposal, companies that are involved in large scale hauling, companies that are involved in large landfill operations, have become increasingly interested in the hazardous waste disposal business" (National Association of Attorneys General, 1979: 102). In fact, unless something was done rapidly, Stier claimed that "traditional organized crime elements" would for all intents and purposes control the hazardous waste industry.

Futhermore, in his remarks at this seminar, Stier related that about two and one-half years before (which must have been in the spring of

1977) he first became cognizant of at least the possibility of organized crime figures and companies in the solid waste industry spilling over into the field of toxics. How he became aware is itself of some interest.

> The only people who were at all aware of the problem were the people who were directly involved in the regulation of the solid waste industry, the people in the state Department of Environmental Protection, the people from EPA, and the Deputy Attorneys General who are assigned from the Division of Law in New Jersey to represent the Department of Environmental Protection. Nobody outside of that small group was talking about this problem. I received a telephone call from a public utilities commissioner in New Jersey who said to me that one of his inspectors wanted to go onto a landfill site to conduct an inspection to see whether or not they were dumping toxic waste. And, he wanted me to provide State Police protection for this inspector to go onto the site. I couldn't imagine why in the world a PUC inspector would require State Police protection. As he began to describe what his inspectors had been finding in the northern New Jersey area in the inspection of landfill sites, the scope of the problem began to emerge [National Association of Attorneys General, 1979: 3].

Briefly put, what Stier says they found were numerous gross examples of toxic waste dumping in northern New Jersey by haulers with the cooperation of landfill operators. Nevertheless, Stier adds that following the dictates of the Department of Environmental Protection his officers began their investigations of haulers only. Surely it is important to note that in this area his report to the attorneys general is consistent with his article for Battelle. But his autobiographical excursion does make the decision of the Division of Criminal Justice to concentrate exclusively on haulers more problematic. In the Battelle article this decision flowed from DEP, which alone had special knowledge of this situation and could therefore structure any investigation, at least for a while. Now it is clear that at least some of his officers in Criminal Justice had knowledge of the waste industry in general and that his own introduction to toxics came via the Public Utilities Commission (PUC) and the problems associated with landfills.

THE MANNER OF PRESENTATION: JOHN FINE

At the same meeting in Scottsdale, Arizona, in which Stier discussed toxics, John Fine, who at the time was an Assistant Attorney General in charge of an Organized Crime Task Force in the state of New York, also gave a presentation on hazardous waste. According to Fine, the problem of illegal hazardous waste disposal was not a white-collar crime issue, but rather one of organized crime. He stated, for example, that police investigations "indicated that racket figures in northern New Jersey were openly boasting that they had a waste disposal landfill just over the border in New York" (National Association of Attorneys General, 1979: 8). After receiving that information sometime in 1977, the New York Attorney General's office started an investigation into illegal disposition of hazardous wastes.

Continuing, Fine related the difficulties encountered by the local sheriff when he began probing into what turned out to be two landfills in his county that were receiving hazardous wastes and were controlled by organized crime figures. For example, "the sheriff's deputies were run off the road, police officers were threatened with guns and city employees who were attempting to enforce the city ordinance had their families threatened" (National Association of Attorneys General, 1979:9). Moreover, it turned out that considerable political pressure was brought to thwart the investigative efforts. Among the ways this was manifested included the cutting off of funds "to the sheriff's investigative department, the detective bureau" by certain county legislators; threats by "town officials" directed to the local police chief and his officers if they participated with the sheriff in his investigation of the landfills; and the sponsoring by one of the landfill owners of a rival candidate for sheriff in an upcoming election (National Association of Attorneys General, 1979: 9).

As the investigation and attendant problems continued, other factors emerged. A contractor who had successfully but unwisely underbid others for a town contract to provide landfill cover had his house torched. Intriguingly, Fine added, "the local New Jersey police department called the fire accidental, but fire inspectors found accelerant used at two different points in his home and declared it to be arson" (National Association of Attorneys General, 1979: 9). Following the fire, the contractor surrendered and his landfill operation was taken over by an organized crime figure. To indicate further the degree of corruption and terror, Fine described one meeting he had with the regional director for the New York Conservation Department. The regional director would meet with Fine only at night with all the window blinds drawn.

One final example from Fine's talk concerning the extent of public corruption flowing from organized crime's involvement in the hazardous waste industry emerged when Fine went to Washington, D.C. The purpose of his trip was to confer with both Senate and House investigators who were looking into the affairs of the Environmental Protection Agency. Fine states:

> I went into the EPA and spoke with a man who at that time was a high official concerned with hazardous waste assessment. He put his feet on his desk, he looked at me, and he said, "Before we talk, let me tell you this. If you're getting into these matters, these hoods that are involved in this kind of thing can buy a Governor like that" [National Association of Attorneys General, 1979: 9].

Fine summarized the intelligence gathered over the course of his investigation, which moved from the northern New Jersey and adjacent New York area to encompass larger regional areas. He was convinced that "racketeering elements dominate the industry and their desire to reap fortunes from improper disposition of toxic wastes has really destroyed human health and irreversibly degraded the environment" (National Association of Attorneys General, 1979: 9). In addition, he stated that one of the largest toxic waste conglomerates in the United States "had a swindler as its chief executive officer, and racketeers with criminal records as principal operating officers for their subsidiary companies that were picking up and disposing of these waste materials" (1979: 9). That particular company, he continued, has toxic waste disposal sites all over the nation with at least some "deliberately established with limited assets, with undisclosed ownership, and with blind trusts as owners" (1979: 9).

It seems to us that the two interpretations of the nature or type of illegality associated with the hazardous waste industry are fundamentally antipodal. Stier, on the one hand, characterizes the issue as one of white-collar crime, while Fine strongly suggests that the industry is controlled or dominated by organized crime. Futhermore, we claim that the choice of terms is important, with one tending to call forth certain control strategies that are essentially different from what would flow from the other.

It is highly possible, as we stated earlier, that the characterization of criminality in the hazardous waste industry as a type of white-collar crime is deceptive. By that we mean that it is likely to entrap the unwary whose knowledge of the illegalities commited by certain hazardous waste carters and site operators is based on the statements of Stier or of a number of other political figures similarly situated. Probably what makes that material most insidious is that it slyly diverts attention from the politics of organized crime. As John Fine noted in his talk on toxics, one of the most pervasive and perverse features of the situation in New York and northern New Jersey was the degree to which organized crime figures were represented by local politicians. That is, of course, also the chilling message delivered to Fine by an official of the EPA. Political corruption is the handmaiden of organized crime and not some episodic feature found only by culling the literature on governmental deviance. And it is precisely here, with the issue of political corruption, that the actions and activities of New Jersey law enforcement have been most suspect, if not outright derelict. This is not to suggest that New York has been any better investigating the inevitable political corruption that is so deeply intertwined in the hazardous waste industry as structured by organized crime. For all John Fine's investigative zeal and determination, his reward from the state of New York was his termination of employment. Nevertheless, it is New Jersey which has claimed to be leading the fight against illegal hazardous waste, and it is former Director Stier who has placed himself on the public record as to the extent and nature of criminality in the hazardous waste industry.

SOME MISSING LINKS

We noted earlier that in former Director Stier's article for Battelle he went on to discuss ways out of the organizational or institutional dilemma that plagued New Jersey's fight against the illegal hazardous waste industry. In fact, Stier states that New Jersey found a solution to the myriad problems of toxic waste enforcement. The answer came, he writes, with the creation of the New Jersey Inter-Agency Hazardous Waste Task Force, which is composed of "representatives from the civil and criminal justice divisions in the State Attorney General's Office, the United States Attorney's Office, the State Department of Environmental Protection, and the United States Environmental Protection Agency (EPA)" (Stier, 1980; 189). Also cooperating with the above, Stier adds, are elements of the state police and the Office of the Medical Examiner.

This formidable array of environmental and enforcement agencies, guided by established management principles and topped by a Hazardous Waste Advisory Commission, provide the coordination and cooperation necessary to overcome the problem. It is more than worth noting at this juncture that after presenting these institutional changes, Stier finishes his essay negating a principle or issue he had himself raised in his paper in a section titled "Existing Remedies and Their Use" (1980: 173). In that section, Stier remarked on the usefulness of RICO legislation in the struggle against white-collar crime. RICO, which stands for Racketeer Influenced Criminal Organization, originally emerged from the Organized Crime Control Act enacted in 1970 (Neuenschwander, 1981; Block, 1980). Stier's earlier comments on RICO note that "the underlying theory of RICO is that civil and criminal liability will arise out of a criminal business enterprise or a legitimate business taken over or supported by financial resources which are derived from criminal activity" (Stier, 1980: 174). And a successful RICO prosecution would provide punishments "such as fines, imprisonment, and criminal forfeiture of the defendant's interests in the enterprise." Also, prosecuting under RICO could "result in civil orders of divestment, prohibitions against business activities, and orders of dissolutions or reorganization." Finally, and perhaps most significantly, Stier writes that conviction under RICO enables "victims" to sue to recover treble damages (1980: 174). What Stier has to say about the usefulness of RICO at the end of his essay is this: "We must carefully evaluate our alternatives. For example, RICO statutes may be counterproductive if they broaden law enforcement remedies and thereby discourage interagency cooperation" (1980: 192).

There is, of course, absolutely no way of knowing exactly what Stier means by this caution. Nowhere in the essay are there examples of the inutility of RICO; nowhere are there examples of RICO prosecutions causing the dissolution of agency cooperation. It may well be that this aside stems from some real and palpable problem experienced in New Jersey law enforcement. But without any discussion in the text, it simply cannot be assumed. What may be assumed, on the other hand, is that this caution about using RICO, especially in cases arising from the hazardous waste investigation, provides us with another instance in which the linking of organized crime and the toxic waste industry appears to be anathema in official circles in New Jersey. To buttress this point, let us note that in the many indictments and several prosecutions stemming from the waste investigation in New Jersey, not one has employed RICO.[2]

More important, however, than using RICO or not is that the official presentation of the illegalities rampant in the hazardous waste industry as a variant of white-collar crime has served to limit New Jersey's investigations. Linking the problem of toxic wastes to the amorphous inventory of white-collar offenses instead of to organized crime has helped to steer investigations and investigators away from the links between known organized crime figures involved in the toxic waste industry and what appear to be their upperworld patterns, patrons, and protectors.[3] Moreover, one might argue that the centralization of investigative efforts praised by former Director Stier as a way out of the muddle could just as well be a method of limiting investigative efforts.[4]

There is a somewhat tired truism about social problems that is, we think, nevertheless appropriate to resurrect at this time. It holds that those who are able to define a social problem can, to some extent at least, control it. This notion takes on a sinister tone if it can be shown that the control function is employed to deceive or for other iniquitous purposes. In such instances, it becomes clear that those who have the power to define must themselves be carefully scrutinized. We realize, of course, that in general the application of one particular label or definition to a type of criminality in a few criminological publications is not the full measure of the power to define. But in the particular case under discussion, the fact that the definition of criminality in the hazardous waste industry as white-collar crime has been advanced by the Director of Criminal Justice in New Jersey, that state which, to reiterate, has supposedly led the fight most forcefully against the illegal disposition of hazardous wastes, the state which has had, reportedly, over $6 million in both EPA and LEAA grants used to pay for the creation of the Hazardous Waste Task Force and its subsequent investigations, adds an unfortunately significant degree of credibility to the definition. One concrete expression of this power to define was given informally by officials in the U.S. Department of Justice. Contacted on an informal basis about the possibilities of funding research on organized crime's control of the hazardous waste industry in the northeast, the reply given was that the illegalities had little to do with organized crime. Clearly, the Department of Justice, through LEAA, had invested substantial research funds[5] in New Jersey's activities and was either convinced by New Jersey that the crime was white-collar criminality and not so-called "traditional" organized crime criminality, or did not care to sponsor research that might display that earlier funding produced less than accurate results. Whatever the particular reasons, the fact is that the Department of Justice incorporated the criminological assumptions advanced by New Jersey. And, as all social science researchers know, the assumptions of funding agencies have an enormous impact on what is researched and, therefore, on both the academic and public perceptions of social problems.

THE REAL EMPIRICAL BASE

There are two issues left to discuss. The first is what may appear to be the quasi-conspiratorial tone of our essay. What we have been suggesting implicitly is that public officials in New Jersey—most especially Edwin Stier—have structured in various ways a false criminology. By this we do not mean to imply that Stier and other New Jersey officials set out to subvert criminology inquiry because of some notion that academic criminology is in itself an important and powerful agent. Instead, it appears to us that Stier's presentations, as well as other documentary efforts produced by the Hazardous Waste Task Force, have become incorporated into the criminological discourse simply through a type of academic inadvertence. Thus far, statements that are highly critical of the thrust of current investigations and the manner in which they have been conducted have appeared largely in publications with very limited circulation (Ironbound Committee Against Toxic Wastes, 1981) or in newspapers that do not have a national readership (Jaffee, 1980, 1982) and are thus routinely ignored by researchers. This, coupled with the disinclination to engage in long-term and difficult field research without major funding, has resulted in the apparent elevation of publications such as Stier's Battelle article into one of the major interpretive essays on the topic.

While we are not accusing Stier and others of attempting to subvert academic inquiry, we are claiming that they certainly appear to have ignored the major facts concerning the illegal hazardous waste industry. We base this claim entirely on what is and has been available in reports, hearings, intelligence files, and other types of documentary evidence developed over time by law enforcement and legislative bodies in New Jersey itself. For example, since at least 1959, New Jersey officials have known that the solid waste industry has been illegally managed and controlled by career criminals, individuals with long-standing ties to major traditional organized crime syndicates (New Jersey State Senate, 1959). In addition, there is ample evidence that many of these same individuals are precisely the ones who most rapidly entered and for all intents and purposes rapidly became the core of the hazardous waste industry. Even the most elementary analysis indicates this inescapable fact. Moreover, in the plenitude of material on the waste industry in general, one major finding consistent for the past 24 years or so is that political corruption is a mainstay of the system. Consider in this regard the following passages from Robert Greene's story of Abscam, called *The Sting Man* (1982: 175-176):

Senator Williams, Weinberg knew, was a total creature of the New Jersey Democratic organization, one of the most corrupt political parties in the country. Good and some of the other FBI agents had given Weinberg a sketchy outline of the system. Errichetti and other New Jersey politicians were completing his education.

The New Jersey Democratic organization, which the Senator represented, had been molded in 1949 as an alliance between the party and the mob by former party boss John V. Kenny of Jersey City. Kenny had shaped and ruled the party for nearly twenty-eight years. While he held power, the state was for sale. The mob moved at will . . . . he had set the tone of interaction between mobsters and politicians for years to come.

While reciting this history of New Jersey corruption, Greene introduces a pivotal individual named George Katz who was a "garbage contractor" and a "known bag man for corrupt officials" (1982: 176). Concerning Katz's well-known past, Green writes:

The aging businessman had become a millionaire through a series of corrupt deals with New Jersey Democratic officials spanning thirty years . . . . Katz had another business edge . . . . He was a close friend of underworld financial wizard Meyer Lansky and Pete La Placa, who at the time was a leading figure in the New Jersey Cosa Nostra. Katz's firm handled garbage collections in Newark, Jersey City and a number of other New Jersey communities. He told Weinberg that he had garnered his municipal contracts by paying bribes to elected officials [1980: 177].

The history of George Katz and the waste industry in New Jersey was exceptionally well known. Not only that racketeers were deeply involved in the industry but that they controlled both waste hauling and, most important, its disposition had been established for quite some time. *The Sting Man*, with its reliance on the Abscam tapes and interviews with Mel Weinberg, only confirmed what had been published in both state hearings into the industry in 1959 and in transcripts released by the FBI in the 1960s, what were called the DeCarlo tapes (recorded in 1962 and 1963) and the DeCalvacante tapes (recorded in 1964 and 1965). The point is that anyone who cared to know about waste, organized crime, and political corruption in New Jersey could hardly avoid knowing the facts. It would have taken an act of will not to know. For example, the correspondence or connection between the solid waste industry and the toxic waste industry could have been seen quite easily by the construction of a simple table listing haulers, owners, operators,

and managers of disposal facilities covering both solid and toxic wastes.
If that had been done, we contend, then the inevitable conclusion
would have been immediately drawn that the hazardous waste industry
was dominated by organized crime. In addition, it would have meant
that political corruption was operating in the hazardous waste industry
to the same degree as in the waste industry in general. And it is this
issue which has been so assiduously avoided, partly by the characterization of the criminality as white-collar. The reason seems obvious: It
is one thing to acknowledge that politicos and mobsters have conspired
on such matters as garbage contracts, but it is quite another to admit
that they have conspired on activities that produce cancer and birth
defects. The enormous public concern with the health hazards of toxic
wastes is sufficient to explain the otherwise inexplicable reticence to
truly characterize and define the problem. What public official loyal
to a party machine is willing to indict members for participating in
schemes whose results are so horrendous? Indeed, what politico is willing to acknowledge that political "business as usual" has produced one
of the most crucial environmental and health problems of this century?
To cover up this individual and systemic culpability, one crucial step
appears to be to keep the problem uncontaminated with discussions
of organized crime. The tone of injured innocence that dominates Stier's
accounting of his own path to awareness and his account of organizational solutions to the criminality of hazardous waste disposal are both,
to put it mildly, deeply suspect. Academic criminologists, we might add
in closing, have an obligation to be wary of explanations by practitioners
who have what are ultimately political jobs.

NOTES

1.   Sutherland's statements, which we have collapsed into the phrase "white collar
crime is organized crime," are, for example, "White collar crimes are not only deliberate; they are also organized"; "the violations of law by corporations are deliberate and
organized crime" (Sutherland, 1949: 219, 233).

2.   Listing and analysis of New Jersey's law enforcement efforts in the hazardous
waste industry are currently being conducted by the authors in conjunction with an investigation by the New York State Senate Select Committee on Crime.

3.   This sentiment was expressed repeatedly in interviews with New Jersey law enforcement personnel in a variety of jurisdictions. At this time, their identities are being protected.

4.   This point was suggested in conversation with several congressional investigators
who have been continually frustrated in their efforts to question key state informants
in their hazardous waste investigations. Among the key informants is Harold Kaufman,

who testified before a congressional committee and was told by New Jersey state officials prior to his testimony not to discuss certain matters concerning corruption. Congressional investigators were also asked not to question Kaufman about political corruption in New Jersey in conjunction with the hazardous waste industry, as that might interfere with ongoing state investigations. At the same time, one of the most knowledgeable state investigators was told by his superiors in the Hazardous Waste Task Force not to engage in so-called conjecture about corruption and organized crime in his testimony before the Congress (this individual's identity is also being protected).

5.   LEAA has made at least four grants to the Division of Criminal Justice since 1976: $375,000 from 9/76 to 3/78 to establish a white-collar crime investigating unit; this was followed by $449,970 in a follow-up for the period 7/78 to 6/79 which was to be used primarily for matters relating to hazardous wastes; $199,995 to establish a Toxic Waste Investigating Unit from 7/79 to 6/80; and finally, $203,883 from 7/80 to 6/83 to fund the Northeast Hazardous Waste Coordinating Committee, which was to cover 11 states and be administered by New Jersey's Division of Criminal Justice.

REFERENCES

BLOCK, A. (1980) "The Organized Crime Control Act, 1970: historical issues and public policy." Public Historian (Winter): 39-59.
———F. SCARPITTI (1982) "Regulation as property; organized crime and the waste industry." Paper presented at the annual meeting of the American Sociological Association.
EDELHERTZ, H. and T. OVERCAST [eds.] (1980). The Development of a Research Agenda on White-Collar Crime. A Report Submitted by the Science and Government Study Center, Battelle Human Affairs Research Centers, to the Community Crime Prevention Division, National Institute of Justice. Washington, DC: U.S. Department of Justice.
GAYNOR, K. (1977) "The toxic substances control act: a regulatory morass." Vanderbilt Law Review: 1149-1195.
GREENE, R. (1982) The Sting Man: Inside Abscam. New York: Ballantine.
Ironbound Committee Against Toxic Waste (1981) SCA: The Solution to the Problem Is the Problem. Available from 95 Fleming Avenue, Newark, NJ 07105.
JAFFEE, H. (1982) "N.Y. mobsters invading Jersey garbage industry." Newark Star Ledger (May 9) 1.
———(1980) "Toxic waste probe casts informant as hero...and villain." Newark Star Ledger (November 16) 1.
KAHAN, J. (1978) "Reporting substantial risks under section 8(e) of the Toxic Substances Control Act." Boston College Law Review: 859-879.
National Association of Attorneys General (1979) Supremacy of Speeches to the Environmental Control and Organized Crime Control Seminars. Organized Crime Control: Special Report.
NEUENSCHWANDER, J. (1981) "RICO extended to apply to wholly illegitimate enterprises." Journal of Criminal Law and Criminology (Winter): 1426-1443.
New Jersey State Senate (1959) Hearings. Committee Created Under Senate Resolution No. 4 (1958) and Reconstituted Under Senate Resolution No. 3 (1959) to Investigate the Cost of Garbage Collection and Disposal. Trenton: New Jersey State Senate.

STIER, E. (1980) "The interrelationships among remedies for white-collar criminal behavior," in H. Edelhertz and T. Overcast (eds.) A Report Submitted by the Science and Government Study Center, Battelle Human Affairs Research Centers, to the Community Crime Prevention Division, National Institute of Justice. Washington, DC: U.S. Department of Justice.
SUTHERLAND, E. (1949) White Collar Crime. New York: Holt.
U.S. House of Representatives (1981) Organized Crime Links to the Waste Disposal Industry. Hearings before the Subcommittee on Oversight and Investigations of the Committee on Energy and Commerce (May 28). Washington, DC: Government Printing Office.
WILHEIM, G. (1981) "The regulation of hazardous waste disposal: cleaning the Aegean stables with a flood of regulations." Rutgers Law Review 33: 906-972.
ZENER, R. (1977) "The Toxic Substances Control Act: federal regulation of commercial chemicals." Business Law: 1685-1705.

Doris Cubbernuss
Denison University

Beti Thompson
Pacific Lutheran University

7

CORPORATE RESPONSIBILITY
Some Implications of the Ford Pinto Case

In recent years, there has emerged an increasing concern with the control of corporate crime. The consequences of some corporate crimes are tremendous in terms of their economic, physical, and social impacts on societies and their members. The issue of controlling corporate crime has typically been addressed within a legalistic framework; that is, the responsibilities of corporations have been defined by the legal and administrative systems and have been limited to those defined by law and/or administrative edict. Implicit in this view is the idea that legal and social responsibilities are synonymous; that is, since laws ostensibly reflect the consensually defined values of societal members, the legal system embodies the societal view of social responsibility. Some social scientists (e.g., Yankelovich, Chambliss, and Quinney), however, question the validity of controlling corporate crime within the legal system. In their view, the interrelationships between interest groups and the law-making process preclude value consensus and tend to produce laws that are favorable to certain groups at the expense of others. Chambliss (1971) argues that the state (which is part of the law-making and law-enforcing system) cannot be value free, either in the enforcement of law or the creation of law. He finds the origin of law not in some natural order or consensus, but in certain interest groups that

AUTHORS' NOTE: Order of authorship is alphabetical and should not be construed as an indication of unequal contribution to this chapter.

121

are closely connected to the political and economic structure of society. "[E]very detailed study of the emergence of legal norms has consistently shown the immense importance of interest-group activity, not
the public interest as the critical variable in determining the content
of legislation" (Chambliss and Seidman, 1971: law 73).

Chief among the groups lobbying for power in the law-making and
enforcement process are corporations. In an oligopolized market of
giant multinationals, the power of such organizations has become
magnified, so much so that John Powers, a corporate executive for
Pfizer's, stated that the multinational corporations are "agents of
change, socially, economically, and culturally" (Barnett and Mueller,
1974: 31). The power of corporations extends beyond the economic
sphere; it delves into the social, cultural, and—most important—
political aspects of human life. There no longer exists a sharp demar-
cation between the public and private sectors. The implication is,
especially in a capitalist society, that the private sector has all the rewards
of being private but few of the responsibilities. The ideal separation
of public and private sectors does not exist in reality; rather, corporations are involved in shaping the political, economic, and social climate
of society.

Corporate involvement in the public sector must result in a questioning of the validity of using the legal system to control corporations.
Corporations, as complex organizations, present specific and unique
problems for the systems of control that have emerged. The organizational nature of corporations and the distribution of power between
corporations and controlling agencies presents a series of impediments
to the control of corporate crime. These impediments may be structural; that is, based in the structure of economic and political arrangements of society (Best and Connolly, 1976), or bureaucratic. If
the impediments are structural, the ideological legitimacy of the power
of controlling agencies is threatened.

STRUCTURAL IMPEDIMENTS

Structural impediments involve those characteristics of the prevailing political-economic relations in society that mitigate against effective control of corporate powers by legal control organizations.

Best and Connolly (1976) cite the increasing inability of the capitalist
system to meet the needs of the less powerful individuals and organizational actors in the society because of the commitment of state interven-

tion into the economy to promote the process of capital accumulation in the private sector. Miliband (1969) argues that the state system (government, administration, regulatory organizations, etc.) has a fundamental commitment to capitalism and that this commitment limits actions. Government intervention in business affairs is geared to the purpose of helping the capitalistic enterprise; for example, the costs of research and development are prohibitive for small industries, and even large businesses depend on state support (through the public sectors of the military, communications, federal grants, etc.) to subsidize their research and development. Arguing that the interdependence of public institutions and private business or political economy became permanent after World War II, Epstein (1966) identifies a number of developments "relevant to an understanding of the changes in recent patterns of corporate political involvement" (p. 38). Among these are official government roles in maintaining economic stability, an increase in military and foreign expenditures, an increase in federal economic activity, and enormous costs of technological development that have resulted in collaboration between government and business. Because of the resultant political economy, corporations are able to act effectively in the political arena. Legitimate political involvement on the part of corporations may serve as a structural impediment to effective control of corporations, since corporations are often the major beneficiaries of the state's commitment.

The legal system in American society is not immune from influence by the political economy. Criminologists have been concerned with the unquestioned acceptance of the law as an arbiter of behavior. In a society based on capitalist economic relations, with a state system committed to the preservation of those interests, justice, or law, will also be "inevitably shaped by social reality: it is an integral part of the social, economic, and political structure of society" (Quinney, 1980: 6). Law, then, should not be perceived as necessarily reflecting common social concerns nor advancing values important to all members of society. Quinney (1975), for example, argues that law tends to preserve existing systems rather than to reflect the wishes of the public. Platt (1975) adds that it is not feasible to "accept the fiction of neutral law" (p. 103). Goff and Reasons (1980), in an empirical examination of Canadian anti-combines laws, determined that laws support "the general interests of capitalism" (p. 136).

Despite the economic influence on the law-making process, "justice" in the control of corporations refers primarily to corporations' adherence to formal laws. Societal actors are so accustomed to using law as a standard for behavior and for justice that questioning of the *substance* of justice seldom occurs. "Justice is in its turn reduced to the actual laws" (Marx, 1972: 80). As Quinney points out, however, this

> leaves wide open such questions as the concrete meaning of equality, the social reality of equality and inequality, the existence of class conflict and state power, and the struggle for a better society beyond a narrow sense of justice [1980: 7].

To the extent that law is concerned with prevailing economic relations and promotes the interests of corporations, Quinney's concerns are unlikely to be addressed.

Parenti (1980) identifies several characteristics of the American economy that contribute to corporate irresponsibility and the inadequacy of the extent to which justice is a consideration in the control of corporations. The concentration of economic power among a relatively small number of social actors, the dominance over political power (especially in terms of control over major institutions) of the major corporations, and the promulgation of an individualistic ideology that results in the privatization of public wealth, an emphasis on consumption rather than need fulfillment, and denial of responsibility for others in society are among them.

Stone, in analyzing the growth of corporate influence, attests to the autonomy of the corporation from the general society and their demands. "Increasingly, the corporation could operate where it wanted to, grow to whatever size it wanted, manufacture any products, and provide any services it chose" (1975: 22). The ineffectiveness of the government against corporate power is reflected in Marcus' conclusion that "corporate power remains essentially unchecked, and is likely to remain so in the forseeable future" (1977: 100-101). The autonomy of the large corporations means that it need not be responsive to the public interest, either in terms of social costs or social needs, and that corporations are relatively immune to outside control.

BUREAUCRATIC IMPEDIMENTS

The inadequacy of capitalist formulations of justice is acute when the problem of control of corporations is considered. The reliance of corporations on the formal rationality of the law for definitions of corporate responsibilities is an indication of the narrow conception of justice utilized in the relations between state control organizations and economic corporations. Bureaucratic impediments to the control of corporations revolve around an emphasis on rationality in organizational decision making. Ladd (1970) emphasizes that organizations are structured by specific goals whose attainment is possible through organizational processes. Utilizing Weber's ideal type description of bureaucracy in action, Ladd notes that organizations are a "language-game model" of decision making. The purpose of the model is to point out that decision making occurs within a specific environment; that is, certain "rules" determine what is to be done and the scope of alternatives. In the case of formal organization, the rule is rationality.

Rationality requires, among other things, the predictability of outcomes. A typical rational predictive device is cost-benefit analysis. An example may be illustrative. The Ford Motor Company demanded the rapid production of a compact car when it perceived its share of the market threatened by imports (Dowie, 1977). Upon discovery of a serious defect in the Pinto (Ford's answer to the imports), Ford conducted a cost-benefit analysis of the problem—a practice that is common in an industry regulated by rationality. Setting a value on human life and calculating the estimated lives to be lost or injuries to occur versus the cost of correcting the defective fuel system, the cost-benefit analysis showed greater profitability in continuing to manufacture the automobile and "pay off" survivors and their families, than in recalling, correcting, and/or retooling the fuel system of the Pinto (from Ford Internal Memorandum cited in Dowie, 1977: 24).

Sutton and Wild (1979) also noted that rationality is the key for large organizations. They argue that corporations rationally *need* to shape and control decision making in order to meet their goals. "The extension of exact calculation in the economy, the subjection of work and social life for precise regulation, and the codification of norms into formal laws are examples of this process" (p. 187). They go on to note that this rationality requires formal law so that outcomes may be carefully predicted. The emphasis on rationality is prevalent both within organizations and in organizational interaction within their environment. The legal system, as a predictable, written set of rules, provides a rational definition of corporate responsibilities. The dependence of corporations on the formal rationality of the law is an indication of the extent to which definitions of social responsibility have been narrowed to the legal responsibilities of corporations. Sutton and Wild (1979) point out the problem with such an approach:

Where judicial formalism prevails, the judge concentrates solely on applying preexisting rules based on logic. "Whatever facts remain undisclosed in the course of this procedure do not exist as far as the judge is concerned." According to Weber the judge "aims at establishing only that
relative truth which is attainable within the limits set by the procedural
acts of the parties." Consequently, substantive injustice may occur under
a formally rational system of law [pp. 188-189].

The problem, then, in terms of the responsibility of corporations,
is twofold: (a) structural impediments that result in a formalized legal
system that favors corporations, and (b) formal rationality that may
lead to an omission of substantive factors in deciding court cases of
corporate responsibility. The emphasis on formal rationality makes it
possible for the specific "nonresponsible" aspects of corporate activities
to be ignored in the administration of the law. This, coupled with the
structural impediments to justice, defines corporate responsibility in
ways that may be quite incongruent with social responsibility.

An Example of Impediments to Justice

A recent criminal court case, Indiana v. Ford Motor Company (1980),
illustrates the inadequacy of using the criminal justice system to control corporate behavior. In this landmark case the Ford Motor Company, as a corporation, was indicted by a grand jury who charged that
Ford "did recklessly authorize and approve the design and did recklessly
design and manufacture a certain Pinto automobile, Serial
Number F3T10X298722F, in such a manner as would likely cause said
automobile to flame and burn upon rear-end impact"
(Indictment, 1978: 1). The Ford Pinto affair provides insights into both
the structural and bureaucratic impediments to justice.

In terms of structural impediments, the interrelationships of the automobile industry and the political process are indicated in a number
of ways. U.S. Secretary of State William Rogers (1971) told executives
of large corporations, including Ford, that "the Nixon administration
is a business administration. Its mission is to protect American business"
(The Ford Motor Company, 1978: 6). In return (as it were), Ford contri-
buted to the Committee to Re-elect the President (Nixon) a sum of
$133,441. Of this, $102,776 was a secret contribution. Of the total Ford
contribution, $49,776 was a personal contribution from Henry Ford
II (Aspin, 1973: 3). The press release from Congressman Les Aspin
(D-Wisc) noted the "solid evidence of the endless trade-off between
big business and the Pentagon" (Aspin, 1973: 3).

The above is not surprising in view of interlocks between Ford and the political system. Robert McNamara, for example, held various executive positions at Ford from 1946 to 1961. In 1961 he was appointed Secretary of Defense. Douglas Toms, who headed NHTSA (National Highway Traffic Safety Administration) from 1969 to 1973, is now the president of a recreational vehicle company which does "substantial business" with Ford.

A further example of the interrelationship of the automobile industry and the polity came to light in a document concerning White House involvement in the regulation process. This memo "sets out the statement of the White House concern for the air bag and other regulatory burdens on the auto industry" (Heffelfinger, 1971). The memo refers to the RECAT (Regulatory Effects on the Costs of Automotive Transportation), which addresses the question, "How far can and should the government enter into regulation and establishment of standards for automotive design and inspection?" (Heffelfinger, 1971). The memo suggests that active White House involvement in weakening regulatory power is occurring.

As a partial result of the political pressure, the NHTSA was relatively inactive in terms of establishing safety standards. In a 1968 communication, Ralph Nader wrote:

> The Bureau must take increasing care that the companies do not make laughing-stocks out of already anemic levels of production safety. The Bureau was not established to lag behind one, two, or more years, but to lead, repeat, to lead [Nader, 1968].

Again in 1973 the DOT (Department of Transportation) was taken to task for its slowness in responding to safety measures. Congressman John Moss (D-Calif) talked of "adding amendments to pending motor-vehicle legislation, if DOT fails to act" ("Fiery Car Collisions," 1973: 8). In 1976 the Oversight and Investigation Committee of the House Commerce Committee sharply criticized NHTSA for "the virtual halt of the federal motor vehicle safety program over the last two years" ("Virtual Halt," 1976: 1). Noting the provision in the National Traffic and Motor Vehicle Safety Act of 1966 for comments on proposed rules, the subcommittee stated, "the vast majority of written comments on proposed rules, the subcommittee stated, "the vast majority of written comments are submitted by the regulated industry" ("Virtual Halt," 1976:1). The subcommittee also accused NHTSA of bowing to "increased resistance from industry," thus losing effectiveness. In addition, the subcommittee chided that the lack of NHTSA action was also due to "political interference in NHTSA rule-making by the White House Domestic Council, the Office of Management and Budget, and others" ("Virtual Halt," 1976: 2).

The Ford Motor Company was especially active in shaping the legal environment concerning automobile safety. Especially pertinent to the impediments to justice were its actions in (a) response to the proposed National Traffic and Motor Vehicle Safety Act of 1960 and (b) Ford's lobby efforts in response to Standard 301 (the federal standard for fuel system integrity).

Ford's Lobby Efforts Against the Safety Act. The CIS report on the Ford Motor Company summarizes Ford's response to the National Traffic and Motor Vehicle Safety Act:

> People who know him cannot remember Henry Ford II taking a stronger stand than the one he took against the regulation of safety design.
>
> By 1965 most pundits and lobbyists saw the handwriting on the wall and prepared to accept government "meddling" in the last bastion of free enterprise (the automobile industry). Not Henry. With bulldog tenacity he held out for defeat of the legislation to the very end, loyal to his grandfather's invention and the company that makes it. But the Safety Act passed the House and Senate unanimously and was signed into law by Lyndon Johnson in 1966.
>
> While lobbying for and against legislation is pretty much a process of high-level backslapping, press-conferencing, and speech-making, fighting a regulatory agency is a much subtler matter. Henry Ford II headed home . . . and a planeload of the Ford Motor Company's best brains flew to Washington to start the "education" of the new federal auto safety bureaucrats.
>
> Their job was to implant the official industry ideology in the minds of the new officials regulating auto safety. Briefly summarized, that ideology states that auto accidents are caused not by cars, but by (1) people and (2) highway conditions ["The Ford Motor Company," 1978: 44].

Henry Ford II continued to oppose government interference in the area of automobile regulation. In a 1969 speech to the Harvard Business School, he argued that the "danger of losing our business freedom is greater than ever" ("Ford Sees Danger," 1969: 6) and added that Ford is "now spending $500,000 a year in the United States and Canada to keep up with government standards and catch up with public expectations with respect to automobile safety and air pollution" ("Ford Sees Danger," 1969: 6).

Ford's involvement in shaping the regulatory environment is also suggested in press reports surrounding the 1973 RECAT report. As previously mentioned, the committee that produced RECAT recommended that careful examination be paid to the costs of regulation within the auto industry. The role of Ford in the initiation of the RECAT committee was disclosed (or at least suggested) by the Center for Auto Safety:

> Ralph Nader's CAS questions the curious sequence of events that occurred about the time the study began. Last April 27, accompanied by Ford Motor Company President Lee Iacocca, Henry Ford II met with President Nixon to discuss "matters relating to the auto industry." Ford denies suggesting RECAT, but two days later a White House memorandum circulated through various Federal departments proposing a cost study. Now, shortly before oral arguments on the airbag regulation are scheduled to begin in Cincinnati Federal Appeals Court, RECAT pops up. This week, Iacocca said, "the report comes none too soon" to show the dangers of boosting consumer costs without carefully considering the nation's economy ["A Backlash", 1972: 23].

Lobby Efforts Against Standard 301. Standard 301 was first proposed in 1967 but was not finally approved until 1975 with implementation required in September 1976. During this time Ford was actively involved in providing information into the rule-making process.

Ford's actions and motives in delaying the standard have been addressed in court. Hews, for example, in Grimshaw v. Ford, states:

> The next document is entitled "Fuel System Integrity Program Financial Review". . . . I bracketed a portion on page 2 which points out in the document . . . that it was company policy to delay any fuel tank changes until forced to adopt them by a law established by the government and to do everything to delay that law as long as possible. No matter what figure you accept, what they did is they took a model and they misrepresented it in its presentation to the federal government in order to delay the passing of 70-20 (Standard 301) and in order to save corporate profits by delaying the passage of the legislation [1977: 6-8].

The manipulation by Ford involves a provision in the rule-making process of NHTSA that requires a period of time following publication of proposed rules, during which comments may be made to the proposed rules. Ford took advantage of this provision a number of times. From the first notice of rule making on November 30, 1970 until the final standard was approved in October 1975, Ford resisted the standard. Some of the objections made to the standard included a zero-fuel-spillage clause, a fixed-barrier impact, the technical difficulties of testing vehicles to meet the standard, and the poor cost-benefit ratio to be obtained by implementation of such a standard. In regard to the last complaint, Ford cited a statement in the NHTSA's Program Plans Books which read, "Approval of rules-making plans is based on a careful analysis of safety payoff in terms of lives saved and reduction in injuries, and estimates of costs to the consumer" (Grush and Saunby, 1973: 2). Ford argued (with corroborative evidence) that the standard yielded extremely poor cost-benefit ratios and should therefore be abandoned.

The manipulation of the legal environment is also greatly enhanced by the bureaucratic characteristics of NHTSA. While the agency has subpoena power (Karr and Apcar, 1979; Nader, 1977) and recourse to civil penalties and injunctions (Bradford, 1978), resistance to the application of standards may be stiff. The long process involved in recall decisions is illustrated by Karr and Apcar:

> Auto-recall decisions, often costly and controversial, don't just happen overnight. Many months of backstage maneuvering may precede the final blow. When a serious safety issue is involved, the process may start with news stories or car-owner complaints; then may come lengthy government investigation and testing, consumer group pressure for government action, resistance by the car's manufacturer, an official finding of a safety defect, and a conflict between the company and Washington over planned repairs [Karr and Apcar, 1978].

The procedural and pragmatic constraints within which NHTSA operates also include its responsibility for performance rather than design criteria in the implementation of standards, the control of pertinent information by the organizations it is attempting to control, and the difficulty in determining adequacy of lead time necessary for the implementation of the standards. Ralph Hitchcock, then acting director of the Office of Crashworthiness Motor Vehicle Program, has attested to the use of performance standards in the case of Standard 301. "Use of [particular] devices . . . in fuel tanks, however, is completely up to the manufacturer of the vehicle. This standard is performance, rather than design, oriented. In other words the manufacturer may use whatever design he chooses as long as the performance requirements are achieved" (Hitchcock, 1977). While this does not necessarily impede the effectiveness of the NHTSA, it can have several implications for the control of corporations. Performance criteria require the crash-testing of automobiles for their evaluation. Performance criteria maintain industry control over the technological developments in safety. Performance criteria severely limit the effect other individuals and organizations could have on the solution to problems of auto safety. Frustration with this situation is expressed by J.R. Doughty, director of the Canadian Bureau of Traffic Engineering, when he says:

> We further understand that the FMVSS are performance rather than design oriented and that the use of specific designs cannot be specified. Therefore, it appears that these manufacturers, on their own volition, chose an unsatisfactory solution which is now being rectified by requiring the motoring public to further risk their lives [Doughty, 1974].

The dependency of NHTSA, on the industry it is mandated to control, for information about compliance with standards also puts the agency at a disadvantage. Information is important in determining the range of possibilities available to auto companies as well as in determining industry efforts to comply with the standards. While the NHTSA investigation of the Pinto case reveals that a variety of sources of information may be utilized, some of the most important data sources are from the auto companies themselves.

A further source of bureaucratic impediments is found in NHTSA's consideration of corporate "timing." The importance of the timing of standards is indicated by its emphasis in the RECAT report on timing the effective date of standards so that implementation is compatible with the cycles of automobile production. The effects of such delays are summarized by Stewart:

> Until joint participation in the rule-making process is completed and a final rule is published, the performance criteria, test procedures, required lead time, etc. are subject to change. Thus it is only upon finalization of the rule that the Administration can:
>
> 1. Determine a reasonable and effective date, and
>
> 2. Expect the automotive industry to initiate necessary production engineering programs.

Upon review . . . we found that approximately 250 different dockets have been opened with proposed rule-making since the adoption of the National Traffic and Motor Vehicle Safety Act of 1966. From this group, 58 standards and regulations have been officially withdrawn. Others remain active pending NHTSA action [Stewart, 1975].

Structural and organizational implications for the control of corporations can be seen in this examination of the interactions between Ford and the NHTSA. The position of Ford within the auto industry and the political and economic resources it commands by virtue of its size and power serve to shield it from outside interference. The susceptibility of Ford to outside control by judicial and regulatory organizations is further decreased by the structural and bureaucratic limit of those organizations; the manufacture of nearly two million defective cars over a period of six years indicates that the impacts of controls are mitigated, to various degrees, by the characteristics discussed above.

The criminal trial of Ford illustrates further how the formal rationality of the law provides constraints on the control of large corporations. The trial, which commenced in January 1980 (after the indictment was twice challenged by Ford and twice upheld) provides many examples of the structural and bureaucratic impediments to justice. The emphasis on the formal rationality of the legal system as a means of determining corporate responsibility was very nicely illustrated during the trial.

The Ford trial began with an attempt by both the prosecution and Ford to delineate the responsibilities of corporations within American society. This was indicated in the questioning of the prospective jurors. Cosentino, the prosecutor, focused on broad standards of responsibility, asking questions and making statements such as these:

Do you believe corporations have a responsibility to abide by the law?

Do you believe corporations have the same responsibilities as you and I?

Do you know how to define reckless behavior? The jurors must decide if behavior is a substantial deviation from acceptable standards of conduct.

Society creates corporations. Society has a right to govern their conduct. Do you agree?

Do you think corporations have a right to make a profit at the expense of safety?

Do companies that manufacture a defective product have the responsibility to inform consumers? [Trial notes, January 7, 1980].

The prosecution thus attempted to broaden the definition of corporate responsibility to some "acceptable standards of conduct." The Ford team responded with questions that indicated a different view of responsibility:

You must decide the case solely on evidence and the law.

Do you have an opinion about who should decide about these safety features?

Would you consider what Ford did in comparison with other manufacturers?

Would you accept the position that a person might make a mistake and not be reckless?

Are corporations a good influence or a bad influence on society?

Ford desires to maintain a good reputation, right? [Trial notes, January 7, 1980]

The definition of the scope of the case became a constant source of conflict during the weeks of the trial. The issue of corporate responsibility became more and more narrowly defined; that is, more and more congruent with the letter of the law. This trend was especially apparent during the second week of the trial. It was then that arguments were made to limit the evidence.

Ford argued that the jury should not have the right to set standards; rather, the NHTSA, mandated to establish automobile safety standards, had established a 30-mile-per-hour rear-impact standard that should be accepted as an "acceptable standard of conduct." The prosecution rebutted that "there is not now nor ever been standards regarding fuel tank placement on the Pinto, so if Ford strapped the tank to the rear bumper they would not be violating a Federal standard. That can't possibly mean Ford has no responsibility to place it in a safe place. Evidence should be admissible that Ford had a higher state of the art and evidence for standards" (Trial notes, January 14, 1980). Ford made an attempt to define the case on "legal standards" while the prosecution argued for a broader conception of responsibility. In this particular notion Ford was overruled, although the judge noted that he might "reverse the ruling depending on the evidence and facts submitted" (Trial notes, January 14, 1980). In fact, later rulings did prohibit the prosecution from addressing these issues. The issue surfaced repeatedly and the responsibility of Ford became increasingly more narrowly defined.

A major indication of the more narrow focus of corporate responsibility came when Ford sought to limit evidence to the 1973 model Pinto. Although the judge vacillated somewhat, information concerning other Pinto models was generally not admissible into evidence and could not be discussed within the presence of the jury. This approach, while within the letter of the law, neglected the complexities involved in this case. The story of the development of the Pinto, for example, was severely truncated so that pertinent evidence was ignored in the judicial process. The judicial practice of nonconsideration of undisclosed facts (as in the Sutton and Wild formulation) was especially detrimental to the case of the prosecution. The emphasis on the 1973 model resulted in an ahistorical treatment of the case; that is, Ford was able to isolate one product from a broader process of automobile development. This eliminated jury consideration of important facts such as the influence of Ford in shaping the regulatory environment, Ford's prior knowledge of the defect, Ford's state of the art, and Ford's own 1971 analysis of solutions to the Pinto's defective fuel systems.

The ruling limiting information to the 1973 Pinto eliminated much of the evidence the prosecution had intended to present. The prosecution argued repeatedly that the whole story required examination beyond this one product. Regarding the narrowness of the definition, the proscution responded, "There is no such thing as a Montego policy or a Pinto policy. It's Ford policy we're interested in" (Trial notes, January 14, 1980). The prosecution was not able to address Ford policy before the jury because of the limiting rule concerning the 1973 model Pinto. That ruling further eliminated other prosecution documents, such as Ford's cost-benefit analysis of safety features, Ford's own crash tests of Pinto prototypes and early models, the objectives for the Pinto, and more because they did not specifically refer to the 1973 model. In short, "relative truth within limits" allowed only a portion of a much larger phenomenon to be addressed.

The issue of responsibility was further narrowed when Ford was allowed to plead "partially guilty" to the indictment. Ford acknowledged that fire, not the force of the impact, killed the girls driving the car. By making such an admission, Ford effectively argued that the issue was narowed to Ford's duty to warn of the defect. From this time on, argruments such as Ford's reckless manufacture of a defective automobile were virtually irrelevant, since the issue before the court was Ford's duty to warn *after* the NHTSA had determined that a defect existed. The defense consistently addressed this issue. In their view they

were culpable during the 40 days between notice of defect (a legal determination of responsibility) and the particular crash for which they were
being tried. The broader issue of responsibility for manufacturing a
safe product was effectively eliminated. Again, this is a small piece of
a larger story. Evidence exists showing that Ford thwarted the NHTSA
for nearly a year in NHTSA's defect investigation.

By the fifth week of the trial, the issue before the court had become
so narrowly defined that the judge stated that the "issue here is what
caused *this* fire" (Trial notes, February 6, 1980). No information was
allowed into the jury's presence unless it directly referred to 1973
models. Expert witnesses were allowed to testify as to their opinions
but were not allowed to present the documents on which such opinions
were based.

The closing arguments reflected the different views of the law held
by the trial principals. Cosentino again addressed the broader social
responsibility, which he perceived to be the intent of the law:

> Do you know a Pinto blows up if hit at 26 to 28 miles per hour? Do
> you think that's right? If you think that's right, find Ford not guilty and
> they can make more cars just like this in 1980 [Trial notes, March 10,
> 1980].

Ford, on the other hand, expressed the letter of the law:

> This is a criminal case involving 40 days, July 1 to August 10,
> 1978 . . . . The 1973 Pinto met every fuel system standard . . . . We
> did everything we could do to recall the Pinto as quickly as possible [Trial
> Notes, March 10, 1980].

Ford also emphasized rationality in its closing arguments:

> The auto industry is weakened by inadequate capital, massive govern-
> ment control, foreign oil, and competition from foreign manufacturers.
> Ford tried to get into the small car market. Pinto met every standard
> regulation. If the government sets standards and then local prosecutors
> set standards, how can our company survive? [Trial notes, March 10,
> 1980].

The formal rationality of both the law and Ford, a complex organization, functioned to create a definition of corporate responsibility that
was largely ahistorical and very narrow. Within this "relative truth"
and formal rationality, the outcome of the trial was predictable.

CORPORATE RESPONSIBILITY

An important implication of the focus on formal rationality for the control of corporations is that "the very rationality which makes bureaucratic structures effective administrative tools seems to erode moral consciousness" (Jackall, 1980: 356). A narrow legalistic view of corporate responsibilities is incongruent with the powerful positions held by corporations in American society. As Braithwaite and Condon (1979) point out, "contrary to the theory of liberalism, a practical consequence of businessmen rationally seeking their self-interest is that a lot of workers and consumers are needlessly killed and injured" (p. 249).

A view of the corporation as a social and political entity, as well as an economic enterprise, requires that attention be paid not only to legal control of corporations but also to the related issue of corporate responsibility. Dahl (1973) argues that public or social purposes should be served through the chartering of corporations. Implicit in the conception of the corporation as an acting social entity is the moral responsibility of acting organizations (Gross, 1979). Alternative views of corporate responsibility are congruent with alternative views of the legitimacy of corporate powers.

Corporate responsibility may refer to responsibilities to the community, responsibilities to the consumer, responsibilities to employees, responsibilities to stockholders, and responsibilities to society as a whole (Epstein, 1969). The levels of responsibility are further clarified by distinctions among the legal, economic, and social responsibilities of corporations. Although economist Friedman (1977) limits corporate responsibility to profit maximization to help maintain a strong economy, Davis (1977) and Hayes (1977) view corporate responsibility within a broader framework of power. Since corporations, in their view, wield social, political, and economic powers, corporate responsibilities involve legal, social, and economic aspects. Corporate responsibilities, while consistent with the profit maximization motive of organizations in the economic sector, are not limited to economic considerations. Davis proposes that the powers of corporations demand attention to social and legal responsibilities as well as economic responsibilities:

> If business has the power, then a just relationship demands that business also bear responsibility for its actions in these areas. Social responsibility arises from concern about the consequences of business's acts as they affect the interests of others. Business decisions do have social consequences [1977: 182].

The legal responsibilities of corporations are defined by state and federal laws and regulations. The more inclusive view of corporate responsibility reflected in Davis's statement requires not only that corporations not engage in illegal behaviors, but also that they live up to their positions as major social institutions. The definition of the role of the corporation in the alleviation of social costs directly related to the corporation's activities, or in the alleviation of social needs in general, is partly a function of the perceived role of the corporate actor and the legitimacy of corporate activities in political and social as well as economic institutions.

Emphasis on the social responsibilities of corporations is termed by Wendel (1977) "an idea whose time has come." The accountability of the large hierarchically ordered corporations to the public interest, whether responsibility is defined in the more narrow or more inclusive view, has been largely usurped by the organizational rules and goals that concentrate on production and growth. The nebulous nature of societal goals for the American economic system makes them particularly susceptible to the influence of corporate goals, given their greater clarity and consistency. State control processes address the legal responsibilities of corporations within capitalist formulations of justice. Corporate processes are unlikely to promote the social responsibilities of corporations, given the economic and political inequality of societal actors and the inability of the capitalist structure of relations to meet the needs of all members of society. As Sutton and Wild conclude:

> As capitalist societies further develop in complexity, jurists will rely more and more upon abstract formal laws to define minimum rights. Groups pushing for social reforms will likewise see their goals as achieved once legislation is passed. The paradox is that this very proliferation of law, regardless of its content, will tend to confirm existing inequalities. The more formal and complex the body of law becomes, the more it will operate in favour of formal, rational, and bureaucratic groups such as corporations. In one sense, therefore, law and justice may be fundamentally irreconcilable [1979: 195].

REFERENCES

ASPIN, L. (1973) Press release, December 10, Washington, DC.
"A Backlash against New Car Standards" (1972) Business Week, March 25.
BARNET, R.J. and R. MUELLER (1974) Global Reach. New York: Simon & Schuster.
BEST, M.H. and W.E. CONNOLLY (1976) The Politicized Economy. Lexington, MA: D.C. Heath.

138   Career Criminals

BRAITHWAITE, J. and B. CONDON (1970) "On the class bias of criminal violence" in Wilson and Braithwaite (eds.) Two Faces of Deviance: Crimes of the Powerful and the Powerless. Queensland: University of Queensland Press.

BRADFORD, L. (1978) Communication to Dale Johnson, GMC, August 17.

CHAMBLISS, W.J. (1975) "Toward a political economy of crime." Theory and Society 2 (Summer): 149-170.

———and R. SIEDMAN (1971) Law, Order, and Power. London: Addison-Wesley.

DAVIS, K. (1977) "Five propositions for social responsibility," in G. Steiner and J. Steiner (eds.) Issues in Business and Society. New York: Random House.

DITLOW, C.M. (1977) Personal communication to Joan Claybrook, August 23.

DOUGHTY, J.R. (1974) Communication to NHTSA, November 1.

DOWIE, M. (1977) "Pinto Madness." Mother Jones (September-October)

EPSTEIN, E. (1969) The Corporation in American Politics. Englewood Cliffs, NJ: Prentice-Hall.

"Fiery Car Collisions" (1973) The Washington Post, September 20.

The Ford Motor Company (1978) London: Counter-Information Services. (Anti-Report No. 20).

"Ford Sees Danger of Business Losing Freedom" (1969) Automotive News, December 8.

FRIEDMAN, M. (1962) Capitalism and Freedom. Chicago: University of Chicago Press.

"Fuel Fed Fires" (1967) Trial.

GOFF, C.H. and C. REASONS (1978) Corporate Crime in Canada. Englewood Cliffs, NJ: Prentice-Hall.

GRIMSHAW versus FORD (1977) California Civil Action.

GROSS, E. (1979) "Organizations as criminal actors," in Wilson and Braithwaite (eds.) Two Faces of Deviance: Crimes of the Powerless and the Powerful. Queensland: University of Queensland Press.

GRUSCH, E.S. and C. SAUNBY (1973) "Fatalities associated with crash-induced fuel leakage and fires." Ford Motor Company Memorandum.

HAYES, D.A. (1977) "A case for social responsibility," in G. Steiner and J. Steiner (eds.) Issues in Business and Society. New York: Random House.

HEFFELFINGER, W. (1971) OMB Memorandum on regulations pertaining to environment, consumer interest, health and safety. U.S. Government Memorandum, October 21.

HITCHCOCK, R.J. (1977) Communication to E.A. Nickel, September 20.

State of Indiana v. Ford Motor Company (1978) Indictment in four counts charging three counts of reckless homicide, a Class D felony and one count of criminal recklessness, a Class A misdemeanor (September 13).

Interview with Henry Ford (1978) Fortune, September 11.

JACKALL, R. (1980) "Crime in the suites." Contemporary Sociology 9 (May): 354-371.

KARR, A.J. and L. APCAR (1978) "Government pressure propels automobile recalls toward a new high." Wall Street Journal, August 16.

LADD, J. (1970) "Morality and the ideal of rationality in formal organizations." Monist, 54.

MARCUS, S. (1977) "Social responses to corporate power: a condition without a remedy?" in G. Steiner and J. Steiner (eds.) Issues in Business and Society. New York: Random House.

MARX, K. (1972) The German Ideology (C. Arthur, ed.). New York: International Publishers.

MILIBAND, R. (1969) The State in Capitalist Society. New York: Basic Books.

MISCH, H.L.(1977) News release, Ford Motor Company. Dearborn, Michigan, August 29.

NADER, R. (1968) Communication to Wm. Hadden, NHTSA. August 22.

PARENTI, M. (1980) Democracy for the Few. New York: St. Martin's.

"The Pinto Controversy" (1977) The Detroit News, September 3: 4A.

"Pintos, Bobcats Recalled for Gas Tank Problems."(1978) Insurance Institute for Highway Safety Status Report, June 15.

PLATT, T. (1975) "Prospects for radical criminology in the U.S." Crime and Social Justice 1.

QUINNEY, R. (1980) Class, State, and Society. Boston: Little, Brown.

STEWART, F.A. (1975) Communication to James Gregory, NHTSA, January 20.

STONE, C. (1975) Where the Law Ends: The Social Control of Corporate Behavior. New York: Harper & Row.

SUTTON, A. and R. WILD (1979) "Corporate crime and social structure," in Wilson and Braithwaite (eds.) Two Faces of Deviance: Crimes of the Powerless and the Powerful. Queensland: University of Queensland Press.

"Virtual Halt of Vehicle Safety Hit" (1976) Insurance Institute for Highway Safety Status Report, November 2.

YANKELOVICH, D. (1977) "On the legitimacy of business," in G. Steiner and J. Steiner (eds.) Issues in Business and Society. New York: Random House.

ABOUT THE AUTHORS

JAY S. ALBANESE received his Ph.D. from the School of Criminal Justice at Rutgers University in 1981. His most recent books are *Organizational Offenders* (1982) and *Myths & Realities of Crime and Justice* (1983). His current research interests include organizational crime, criminological prediction, and future manifestations of deviance. Dr. Albanese is currently Assistant Professor of Criminology and Criminal Justice at Niagara University.

ALAN A. BLOCK is Associate Professor of Criminal Justice at the University of Delaware. He is the author of *East Side, West Side* (Transaction, 1983) and coauthor of *Organizing Crime* (Elsevier, 1982). He has written numerous articles on organized crime and is currently investigating the role of organized crime in the disposal of toxic waste.

DORIS CUBBERNUSS completed her Ph.D. in 1981 at the Western Michigan University in Kalamazoo. She is currently in the Sociology/Anthropology Department at Denison University in Ohio. Her research interests center on the regulation of large organizations, corporate crime, and international development. A current research project involves an examination of the regulatory process around passive restraint systems in automobiles.

JAMES A. INCIARDI is Professor and Director, Division of Criminal Justice, University of Delaware. He received his Ph.D. in sociology from New York University and has more than twenty years of experience in the clinical and research areas of substance abuse and criminal justice. He is the former editor of *Criminology* and has authored more than 90 articles and books in the fields of criminology, criminal justice, substance abuse, medicine and law.

PETER A. LUPSHA is Associate Professor of Political Science at the University of New Mexico. He teaches and conducts research in the areas of organized crime, political corruption, terrorism, political violence, and intelligence analysis. He is currently conducting research on improving law enforcement intelligence methodologies for combating organized criminal groups and enterprises.

TOM MIECZKOWSKI is currently completing his doctoral dissertation at Wayne State University. He is studying the social organization of narcotics distribution in the Detroit metropolitan community and teaching criminology and sociology at Wayne State and at several other colleges. His area of special interest is organized criminal systems and their description.

JULIAN B. ROEBUCK is Professor of Sociology at Mississippi State University. His research and publication areas are criminology and race relations.

FRANK R. SCARPITTI is Professor of Sociology at the University of Delaware and past-president of the American Society of Criminology (1981). He is the author or coauthor of several books and articles on juvenile deliquency, female criminality, social problems, drug use, and corrections. With Alan Block, he is currently researching the role of organized crime in the disposal of toxic waste.

BETI THOMPSON received her Ph.D. from Western Michigan University in 1981. Ongoing research centers on the role of large organizations and their effects on society; specifically, corporate crime and other forms of organizational deviance. Current research involves an examination of the politics of "airbags." She teaches in the sociology department at Pacific Lutheran University in Washington.

GORDON P. WALDO is Professor of Criminology at Florida State University. He is the author or coauthor of articles on deterrence, discrimination in the criminal justice system, the death penalty, evaluation of criminal justice policies, and other areas of criminology. Current areas of interest include deterrence, research methods in criminology, and criminal typologies.

GERALD O. WINDHAM is Professor of Sociology and Director of the Social Science Research Center at Mississippi State University. His research and publication areas are deviant behavior, substance abuse, and international development.